About This Book

The best cure for abnormal mental attitudes is to get the patient to understand their cause; once he realizes what is wrong with himself and why, he is on the road to recovery. Mr. Parkes uses the same technique in analyzing antisemitism, a very real and persistent form of modern sickness. He estimates that ninety-five percent of the population, including the Jews themselves, are unbalanced on the Jewish question. The Nazis have been defeated but their propaganda persists to some extent in the best-intentioned of us all.

Any minority group suffers certain prejudices from the majority. For historical and sociological reasons the Jews have attracted more of this than any other people: they are a persistent scapegoat for the sins of the world. Mr. Parkes, who knows more about Jewish literature, religion, and laws than most non-Jews, analyzes these factors comprehensively. He traces *The Protocols of the Elders of Zion* from the original Russian forgery to the Nazi version. And he explodes a number of similar myths. By being impartial—by allowing for the distinctive qualities of the Jews, and for the persecution complex that centuries of oppression have engendered in many of them— he presents a rounded picture. He shows that antisemitism is an enemy of the people—not only of the Jews, but of any hope for a better society.

PELICAN BOOKS

AN ENEMY
OF THE PEOPLE:
ANTISEMITISM

BY
JAMES PARKES

PUBLISHED BY
PENGUIN BOOKS, INC.
NEW YORK

Originally published as a Pelican Book by
Penguin Books Limited, England, 1943
Second Printing, 1944

First American Pelican Books edition March, 1946

Penguin Books, Inc., 245 Fifth Avenue, New York 16, N. Y.
Penguin Books Limited, Harmondsworth, Middlesex, England

PRINTED IN THE UNITED STATES OF AMERICA

CONTENTS

Chapter   *Page*

1. TRIAL OF A NEW WEAPON 1
    IN GERMANY 5
    IN AUSTRIA-HUNGARY 11
    IN FRANCE 18
    IN RUSSIA 23

2. THE PROTOCOLS OF THE ELDERS OF ZION . . 32

3. GERMANY OF THE NAZIS 45

4. THE OTHER SIDE OF THE PICTURE 62

5. THE PSYCHOLOGY AND SOCIOLOGY OF
     ANTISEMITISM 82
    THE JEWS AS A MINORITY 91
    THE SOCIOLOGICAL AND PSYCHOLOGICAL PROB-
      LEM OF JEWRY 94

6. JEWISH COMMUNITIES OF THE WORLD TODAY . 111

7. THE ELIMINATION OF ANTISEMITISM . . . 132

BIBLIOGRAPHIES 148

INDEX 150

AN ENEMY OF THE PEOPLE

CHAPTER I

TRIAL OF A NEW WEAPON

A LARGE part of the political history of the 19th century is made up of the struggle, first of the middle class, then of the working class, to secure parliamentary votes, and of the parallel struggle of the representatives whom they elected to secure effective control of the government. In Britain the latter struggle had been won during the previous century, but few people realize how few there were in Great Britain who were qualified to elect representatives to Parliament, especially before the great Reform Bill of 1832. Until then it was only a tiny minority of the people, selected by the hazards of history, not by any special fitness, who had the right to vote. Fifty constituencies returned members, though they had no electors at all, and their owner simply nominated whom he would. One constituency had actually disappeared under the sea; another was a ruined wall, survival of a medieval borough. In Europe the franchise, where it existed at all, was as narrow and as uncertain; and it was only towards the middle of the century that real representation, regularly constituted, began to come into existence. And even then the battle to secure control of the government had still to be fought, and in central and eastern Europe was still not wholly won in 1939.

This fact, that parliaments came into existence without their being intended actually to control governments, probably explains why on the continent the English two-party system never took root. It was a natural development when an executive government had to be found from the House. But so long as the functions of a parliament stopped short at such responsibility, it was more natural for men to fall into the many different groupings which corresponded more exactly to their individual interests.

The emergence of the middle class into the political arena was primarily due to the industrial revolution and to the creation of a new source of wealth and power in the products of industry. It was inevitable that the holders of this wealth should challenge the political authority of the older class whose wealth depended on the possession of land. For, owing to their different needs, industrialists made different demands on governments. The conflict over the wheat laws in England was a good case of this. The landowners wanted high prices for their wheat; the industrialists wanted to keep costs down by cheap bread for their workers. On the continent, where landowners were often semi-independent rulers, they were quite prepared to keep a multiplicity of small states, where each could charge tolls on goods transported across his frontiers. But industrialists wanted large areas with uniform laws and freedom of passage, to enable them to sell their goods as advantageously as possible.

But the middle class was not only an industrial class. In Europe at any rate it was also the class of the intellectuals; and if in England it was largely the industrial interests which compelled the Reform Bill of 1832, in Europe it was largely the intellectuals who caused the series of revolutions which marked the year 1848 in France, Germany, Austria and Hungary. Though these revolutions were all unsuccessful, yet from then onwards the democratic slogans which had first been heard in the French Revolution became part of the political life of Europe, and ideal conceptions of human equality, abstract questions of moral justice, and a general assault on privilege, jostled the increasingly complex demands of industry for the attention of governments and of parliaments.

During this period the electorate was growing in numbers. But it was not necessarily growing equally in education; and political questions were becoming more and more complicated. These complications inevitably involved long and bitter conflict between rival groups with different interests; and in consequence new techniques had to be evolved for securing the favor and votes of the electorate. Governments likewise needed new techniques for winning popular support. For even if a Sovereign, a Chancellor or the President of a Council of Ministers might not be constitutionally dependent on his parliament, it was much easier for him to rule if he could carry a majority of them with him. The success of the techniques discovered was not always proportional to their honesty or their relevance. In fact forgery, deception and red-herrings were discovered to be as capable of winning enthusiastic support, and to have as great vote-catching value, as honest expositions of policy or the intellectual enlightenment of electors.

Even in France, the oldest parliamentary democracy on the continent, the electors could be so completely misled that in 1851 they voted enthusiastically for the abolition of their hard-won rights. In that year Louis Napoleón, nephew of the great Emperor, secured from the eight million voters of the country a majority of nearly seven millions for the abolition of the Constitution, the degradation of Parliament, and the vesting of all power personally in himself. The history of political democracy is shorter, more unstable and more embarrassed than people realize.

This book is concerned with an equally striking but more comprehensive example of the capacity of European electorates to be deceived. There is no better example of this capacity than the emergence and use of antisemitism as a political weapon. There had, of course, been feeling against the Jews among particular classes, or generally among the populace, for many centuries of European history. But it had tended to dwindle in the liberal and 'modern' atmosphere of the 19th century, with its contempt for the superstitions of the past. Where it had survived it was either among the more ignorant of the peasants, or among the more obstinate of those who stood to lose from the developments of the century—the old landowning aristocrats, and the clericals anxious to retain the privileged position of the churches. They hated the entry of the Jews into their 'Christian' society; they hated the democratic, urban, commercial and secular civilization in which the emancipated Jews found themselves at home. And they suddenly discovered that this feeling, rooted both in jealousy and in ancient prejudice, was a most convenient rallying point for those who, from the most diverse points of view, disliked the 19th century; and that it was a most versatile and effective stick wherewith the conservatives might beat the progressives. Political antisemitism had extremely little to do with the Jews as such, just as it had extremely little to do with the real reform of the many evils of the untrammelled industrialism of the century, which the Jews were supposed to control or exemplify. It is necessary to be clear on this point. There *were* serious moral and social problems created by the rapid progress of industry and commerce; there *were* many spiritual and cultural values which were lost, or

4

gravely compromised, by the headlong rush after wealth and material comfort which characterized the period. In addition, the sudden emancipation of the Jews, and the situation of those Jews who still lived a medieval life in eastern Europe, *did* create real problems. But the political antisemitic movement has not to its record a single example of a serious attack upon any of these real problems; in consequence, it has not to its credit any real analysis or understanding either of the Jewish position, or of the evils of the century. Of both it drew an imaginary picture for its own ends. In fact, just as the evils of the century were but a small part of its life, so the reference of the antisemites to actual and precise evils and their reform formed but a small part of their armory; and just as the Jews formed but a minute fraction of the middle classes, so actual Jewish conduct formed but a tiny part of their onslaught on "the Jews." The enemy was "liberalism," "industrialism," "secularism"—anything the reactionaries disliked; and they found by experience that there was no better way of persuading the electors to dislike these things also than to label them "Jewish."

There was also a particular advantage in possessing so comprehensive a weapon in circumstances where both sides of the conflict were made up of alliances and coalitions between various groups. It provided the attackers with a cement to bind them together, in spite of great diversity of interest; it enabled all the enemy to be lumped together under a single head, although they also, in fact, represented all sorts of groups and interests.

In Germany

The scene of its original emergence was the new German Empire created by Bismarck. The year was 1879. Germany had only just realized her unity. It

5

had taken three wars—against Denmark, Austria and France—and all the skill, strategy and lack of scruple of Bismarck, to win this unity out of the kingdoms, dukedoms, principalities, free cities, and what not into which Germany was still divided even after Napoleon had unified, modernized, and co-ordinated the nine hundred odd "states" which existed at the beginning of the century. The conservatives in Germany were those who, in various forms and from various motives, wanted to retain many of these old, almost independent, societies resting on landownership and ancient rights; and the progressives, of whom the most important section was the National Liberal Party, were the party of industry and the big cities, who saw no chance of development so long as the country was divided into so many separate units, each with its own legislation, its own control over expenditure, even its barriers against its neighbors. Industry required a larger field in which to maneuver; raw materials and manpower were not conveniently divided according to the innumerable frontiers which broke up the country. The progressives desired unity largely for the purposes of trade and business development; but there was also a strong group of intellectuals who desired it in order that the German people might take its place among the peoples of Europe as a great cultural and political unit. Bismarck also desired unity, but for the sake of the power of the House of Prussia. For many years the progressives and he worked amicably together. As Chancellor he was not dependent on a parliamentary majority, such as an English Prime Minister would need, for he held his power from above, from the German Emperor, not from below, from the elected representatives of the people; and he even ruled without any parliamentary sanction for his budget for a period of four years. But it was convenient, and on a long view necessary, that his policy should command the support of a majority of the Parliament, and up to 1879 the progressive group had provided this. The weakness of this support was that his motives were not theirs. Though the success of his policy, and the resounding éclat of his three successive victories, had roused a great deal of patriotic fervor, their effect was bound to wear off in time. The business element among the progressives was ultimately more concerned with the development of what was known as 'Manchesterism,' the free trade *laissez-faire* policy under which England had become astoundingly wealthy and the factory of the world. The idealist element among the progressives desired to establish in Germany the responsible, representative, parliamentary government which they admired at Westminster. But Bismarck and his Sovereign, the aged William I, abhorred both Manchesterism and parliamentary democracy, and by 1879 the Chancellor felt strong enough to do without such dubious support. In consequence he set out to disrupt the progressives and destroy their influence.

Now that the Empire was unified and at peace, Bismarck had two immediate objectives. The first was to prevent the transfer of power from the Monarchy to the Parliament, and the second was to secure independent financial resources for the Imperial Chancery, which so far had been dependent on grants made by the separate states out of which the Empire was built up, or on allocations from the Parliament. The best source of this revenue he saw in the imposition of a tariff. In neither of these objects would the progressives help him, but both would be approved or, at least, accepted by two other groups, the various nationalist and conservative elements, and the Catholic elements grouped in the Center Party. Unfortunately none of these were friendly to him.

Bismarck had demanded $1,000,000,000 from France after her defeat in 1870, and France had paid this huge indemnity in less than three years. This vast sum threw German economy badly out of gear. There had been a short period of wild speculation, and then, in May, 1873, an appalling crash. In this crash many of the old landowning class had badly burned its fingers, and, naturally, blamed the government's alliance with the liberal industrialists and bankers for its own follies. And in addition it did not like the secularist, idealist, modernist atmosphere of the new Empire. More serious had been the conflict between Bismarck and the Catholics. In the German Empire which Bismarck had created Protestants outnumbered Catholics by about two to one. The center of the Empire was Protestant Prussia, and the Catholic south and west were consequently inclined to foster separatist tendencies, and to regret the complete exclusion of Catholic Austria from German affairs. Fearing these inclinations, and disliking the political ferment among the Catholics which had followed the Vatican Council of 1870, Bismarck decided to call them to heel. In 1873 he launched a campaign of repressive legislation against them which had no parallel in a 'modern' western European State. This attack—known as the Kulturkampf—lasted for several years, and brought the humiliating spectacle of a modern state persecuting and even imprisoning aged and respected bishops and priests for no more than loyalty to their religion. The Catholics were certainly not likely to be easily won to support the Chancellor.

Now it happened that, as one might expect since the Jews are largely occupied with commerce, there had been some spectacular Jewish bankruptcies in the

crash of 1873; and it happened that among the prominent leaders of the National Liberal Party were two
Jews, Eduard Lasker and Ludwig Bamberger; and it
happened that an important Catholic newspaper of
the Rhineland was in the hands of a fanatical priest, a
predecessor of Father Coughlin, of the name of Augustus Rohling, who was convinced that the Jews were at
the back of everything which at any moment he disliked.

Although nothing particular actually happened in
1879 to bring special attention to the National Liberal
Party, all of a sudden a nation-wide campaign of
extraordinary violence swept Germany of which the
burden was the identification of the Jews with the
National Liberals, and the National Liberals with
everything any good German would avoid.

The actual origins of the campaign have never been
fully explored, but there is little doubt that the mind
behind it was the mind of Bismarck. It was not due to
any hostility to the Jews on the Chancellor's part. He
had been helped in the critical years of his policy by a
section of the Parliament in which there were some
prominent Jews, of whom Lasker and Bamberger were
fairly intimate personal friends; and he had been able
to finance the Austrian war by the aid of a Jewish
banker, Bleichroder. But something had to be done to
discredit the progressives and, as Bamberger himself
says in his memories of Bismarck, "it was typical of his
method that, when a weapon came along which others
had forged for him, he should not let go of it, but keep
it in his arsenal to make use of at a convenient moment
for the discomfiture of his enemy."* Bismarck himself
is reported to have said "I expressed my disapproval of
it, but I did nothing more, as it was a most useful means

_____
*Quoted in *Bismarck und die Juden,* Otto Johlinger, p. 61;
cf. also p. 115.

of attacking the progressives,"* and this pleasant equivocation he communicated to those of his entourage who had relations with the press.

That the launching of an antisemitic campaign had, in Bismarck's mind, nothing to do with the Jews as such is shown by the facts that one of those whom he had invited to frame the imperial constitution which he was now determined to maintain against the progressives, was the converted Jew, Karl Rudolf Friedenthal; that the intellectual founder of the Conservative Party to which he proposed to turn for support was another Jewish convert, Friedrich Julius Stahl; and that the man whom he had chosen to be Minister of Justice in 1879 was a third, Emil von Friedberg. In fact nothing could more clearly show the nature of modern antisemitism than its first emergence. It was a political maneuver which found the Jews useful ammunition, but had no interest in them as Jews.

Having made this discovery, the German conservatives proceeded to develop it vigorously. An Antisemitic League was founded, and the antisemites discovered a leader in a Lutheran Court Chaplain, Adolf Stoecker, creator of the Christian Social Workingman's Union. It mattered nothing to the conservatives that the reason for Stoecker's semi-socialist antisemitism was that the Jews were capitalists, for Stoecker himself sat in Parliament with the conservatives; and it did not disturb Stoecker that the conservatives supported him because they felt that his tepid socialism would be an insurance against the more violent or 'Jewish' form of the disease, represented by Marx and Lassalle. It was an adequate bond of union to regard Jews as the enemy. Antisemitism also helped to bring the second group whose support Bis-

---

* *Ibid*

marck desired to cultivate, the Roman Catholic center, into alliance with the Protestant conservatives. For the Kulturkampf could now be represented as the work of Jewish-led liberal secularists. Indeed Bismarck's lieutenant in executing his anti-Catholic decrees had been a Jewish lawyer, Heinrich von Friedberg. One could forget that he was the brother of the Minister of Justice, and that he had been converted many years previously to Christianity; or, perhaps, one remembered that he had become a Protestant and not a Roman Catholic.

It was altogether a most curious alliance, and it is not surprising that the one thing which it never seriously attempted to do was to produce a policy on the Jewish question. For on this it could never have reached agreement, since its propaganda on the subject was quite incoherent. To Stoecker and the Christian Socialists Jews were an economic class; to Rohling and the Roman Catholics they were a religious group; and to the great historian Heinrich von Treitschke and the conservative intellectuals they were a race. Its real point of union was hostility not to Jewry but to the progressive ideas of liberalism; it mattered little to Bismarck from which gun-site the enemy was discomfited.

If it did not produce a Jewish policy, the antisemitic movement certainly provided German politics during the fifteen years of its existence with an unexpected element of vulgarity, violence and vituperation, and in the dust storms it created the progressives disintegrated and their power disappeared. Germany had to wait until 1918 to make her first unsuccessful essays in parliamentary democracy and cabinet responsibility.

In Austria-Hungary

The same story was repeated in Austria-Hungary, with complications suited to the situation in the dual monarchy. Austria-Hungary was a 'ramshackle empire'

which included within its frontiers Germans in Austria
and Bohemia (the Sudetens), Czechs in Bohemia and
Moravia, Slovaks, Poles in Galicia, Hungarians, and
various groups of southern Slavs. During the whole
period of this story, the empire was ruled by a single
emperor, Franz Joseph, who ascended the throne in
1848 in the middle of the revolutions of that year, and
died in 1916 in the middle of the war which removed
'Austria-Hungary' from the map of Europe.

As in Germany, the developments of the middle of
the 19th century brought an urban, middle-class, liberal, progressive party into prominence and power;
and it was, as in Germany, against this party that antisemitism was directed. But in much more complicated
circumstances. The progressives wanted a modern,
liberal, centralized state with responsible parliamentary government, an idea which cut not only across old
prejudices, as in Germany, but also across the conflicting modern idea of nationalism. For the nationalities
did not want a centralized state, which meant German
dominance; except, of course, the German nationality.
But German conservatives did not want liberalism.
Then Hungary wanted complete independence for
Hungarians, but desired also to dominate her own
minorities from other nationalities. So there the conservatives wanted centralization, and the progressives
federalism, or at least more generous treatment of the
Slav and other minorities. And of course any of the
partners might change places at any particular moment
to conform to some particular figure in the dance of
power. The President of the Council, like the German
Chancellor, was responsible to his Emperor, not to
Parliament, and the same President might, and did,
secure all kinds of different groupings to support him,
by adroit concessions to one side or the other.

In this conflicting medley antisemitism was a most

useful card for the opponents of liberalism. They could agree to it for their own particular purposes, while interpreting it in their own particular way.

The scene actually opens in France, where in 1878 a 'Christian' financier, by name Bontoux, launched the Union Générale as a 'Christian' bank designed to counter 'the international influence of the Jews'; which, in this case, meant the Rothschilds, who had, in fact, passed the zenith of their political influence but were still immensely wealthy. The project was supported by many both of the highest nobility and of the Roman Catholic hierarchy. But it was not long before the shares of the Bank began to depreciate, and finally in 1882 it crashed owing to the speculations of Bontoux, and involved its exalted supporters in ruin. Although there was no evidence that it was more than the speculations of Bontoux which had caused the rapid fall in its shares and its subsequent failure, its victims were easily persuaded that it was Jewish envy and hostility which had led to the loss of their money. One of them was particularly determined to have her revenge. This was the Austrian Archduchess Maria Theresa, wife of the Comte de Chambord, pretender to the throne of France. She was already in contact with an Austrian colleague and counterpart of Bontoux, the Ritter von Zerboni di Sporetti. In 1881 she dispatched him to Germany with instructions to study the technique and activities of the antisemitic movement there. He returned with a mass of literature and ideas. At the same time an Austrian prince of the church persuaded the Imperial Government to appoint the leading, and most venomous, Roman Catholic antisemitic writer in Germany to a Professorship at the University of Prague. This man was Augustus Rohling, who made a specialty of denouncing, not the political or financial activities of 19th century Jews, but the religious pronouncements of the Talmud. He was in no way restrained by the almost total ignorance of Hebrew since, in fact, he did no more than rehash the contents of an immense anti-Jewish work of the early 18th century, the *Judaism Revealed* of Johann Andreas Eisenmenger.

The stage was thus set for an alliance between clericals and conservatives on the familiar model, and it was precisely the support of these groups that the President of the Council at the time desired. With memories of the project of Bontoux they proclaimed their purpose to be the rescue of the soil of Austria from Jewish financiers, and this rallying cry served also to bring in the Catholic Christian Socialists, a party very similar to the Protestant Christian Socialists who formed the backbone of the antisemitic movement in Germany. From Austria Zerboni extended his activities to Hungary, where he was already in contact with a Hungarian member of Parliament, Geza von Onody. It was in Hungary that the first actual battle was fought, a battle which was to strike the keynote of the particular character of political antisemitism in the Austro-Hungarian Empire. The antisemites planned to do no less than revive the medieval accusation that Jews practised ritual murder in order to get Christian blood for their Passover bread. It was a curiously roundabout way of attacking a 19th century liberal, secularist and industrialist section of the population, but it seemed at first that it was going to be successful.

On April 1, 1882, four days before the Jewish Passover, Esther Solymossi, a girl living in Tisza Eszlar, the town which Geza von Onody represented, disappeared. Onody at once proclaimed that the Jews had murdered her for ritual purposes, and had the beadle of the Jewish synagogue arrested. His two children—

aged five and fourteen—were coached with a story of
the guilt of their father which they told the magistrates. Unfortunately for Onody and his friends they
had been careless on details. The children reported
what they had seen through keyholes which could not
be seen through, and so on. The trial looked like
being a fiasco, especially as no evidence could be produced that Esther had been murdered at all; she had
simply disappeared. However the fates appeared to
be on the side of Onody, for shortly afterwards the
body of a girl was found in the river, and the matter
at once came to life again—there were by this time a
considerable number of Jews in prison on Onody's
denunciation. Medical evidence showed that the girl
was several years older than Esther, and her body also
showed no signs of her having been stabbed or bled to
death. Nevertheless, the trial was proceeded with, and
the whole country kept in a state of agitation for some
months. It was more than a year before the absurdity
of the whole matter was publicly exposed by the with-
drawal of the Crown Prosecutor when presented with
the actual evidence; and during all that time the unfortunate Jews were in prison. The final exposure discredited antisemitism in Hungary, but in the meantime an oil painting of the 'murdered' girl was being
publicly exhibited at antisemitic meetings in Germany,
and attracting much attention and sympathy.

While this affair made the antisemites ludicrous in
Hungary, the behavior of Professor Rohling was making them dangerous in Austria. The Professor was
furious at the acquittal of the 'murderers' of Esther
Solymossi, and whenever any occasion offered he demanded to be heard on oath giving proof that the
Jews committed murder for ritual purposes. Austrian
magistrates, however, were largely men of enlightened
minds; and as none could be found anxious to assist the

Professor to perjure himself, he was compelled to un-
burden himself by publishing his views in books and
pamphlets, and especially by reissuing the work which
had originally brought him into prominence, *The Talmud Jew*. This was a hair-raising collection of mis-
translations and inventions, most of which he owed to
Eisenmenger. (Actually when he was finally brought
to book he appeared unable to translate the simplest
Talmudic text himself.) Rohling's *Talmud Jew* kept
the ritual murder accusation alive, and the next move
made by the conservatives was interesting. Out of the
Tisza Eszlar affair they tried to create an antisemitic
party among the Socialists in order to secure a united
'Christian' front of all classes. Relying on the fact that
Austrian workers were to a considerable extent both
ignorant and devout, they employed a paid agitator in
the industrial suburbs of Vienna to stir up antisemitism
among the working classes, on the grounds that rich
Jewish capitalists had secured the acquittal of their coreligionists from the accusation that they had murdered a poor Christian girl. For some months it looked
as though they would succeed. It is the only case during the whole period in which the Socialist party of
any country came near to falling into the trap of believing that 'the Jews' were the enemy which they
should be fighting. But by the courageous intervention
of Dr. Bloch, the Jewish rabbi in the chosen suburbs,
the attempt failed, and was not repeated.

The conservatives then turned to the small traders,
who proved more amenable; and a suitable mixture
of ritual murder and Rohling's Talmud Jew fell on
fruitful soil. In fact it stirred up feelings so violently
that the conservative leader, Count Belcredi, was
summoned by the Vienna police for seeking to provoke
a breach of the peace. Belcredi was acquitted on the
evidence of Rohling—the sworn depositions of the

Royal Professor of Hebrew of the University of Prague were at last heard in court. This acquittal had an unexpected effect. The Jews of Vienna were not particularly pious; they were essentially a middle-class, cultured and emancipated community; and they were completely dumbfounded by the trial and the acquittal. Ignorant of the Talmud themselves, they could not believe that a Royal Professor, who was also a Canon of the Church, could have deliberately given false evidence on oath. They felt themselves compelled to believe that the Talmud *did* contain the awful sentiments and intentions which Rohling attributed to it, and they did not know how to meet the situation. The chief rabbi of Vienna issued a colorless denial, but it had little effect. The Talmud, as interpreted by Rohling, held the stage; and this success of the religious line of attack on the secularist, liberal Jews of Vienna determined the character of Austrian antisemitism for the next ten years. It took two years to bring Rohling himself to book, but it was finally done sucessfully by the same Viennese rabbi, Dr. J. Bloch, who deliberately published such libellous articles on Rohling that he compelled him to bring him to court. But on the day previous to the trial Rohling withdrew the charge, accepted a heavy penalty for costs and thereby admitted the falsity of his statements. But the accusation persisted, and all kinds of ritual murder accusations were made in various parts of Austria for years afterwards, in spite of the fact that, every time a case came to court, it proved impossible to sustain the charge.

During the period 1880 to 1890 the government was supported by a majority of the conservative and nationalist groups together with a large proportion of the clerical elements; and antisemitism was mainly used as an attack on the opposition liberal papers which were largely the product of Jewish journalists. But in

1890 a new coalition including the liberals was formed, and the nationalist and clerical groups changed the nature of their antisemitic propaganda in consequence. In fact, as in Germany, a definite party using the title "antisemitic party" came into being. It was made up of the more intransigent elements of the nationalists together with the Christian-Socialist (*i.e.* conservative) element of the clericals. Its leaders were Prince Lois von Liechtenstein and Dr. Karl Lueger. In 1895, on the eve of the elections, it actually secured the papal benediction on its policy and its newspaper, to the great indignation of numbers of the more moderate and more far-seeing sections of the Roman hierarchy in the country. In the national Parliament the antisemites failed to carry a majority, and they decided to try to carry the elections for the municipal council of Vienna. In this they were so successful that they won two-thirds of the seats. In spite of the indignation of the Emperor Dr. Lueger became Burgomaster of Vienna, a post he held for fourteen years; and it was during the time of his mayoralty, and while antisemitism was one of the main planks of the Viennese elections, that the young Austrian, Adolf Hitler, came to Vienna and formed his opinion on the Jewish question. But the irony of the situation is that what was merely an election device for Lueger became a passionate conviction for his pupil. The former was perfectly prepared to befriend, and to be friendly with, Jews in private while he denounced them on every occasion in public. His antisemitism was an open anti-liberal platform device. His pupil really set out to destroy physically those whom his master so constantly taught him to regard as the most dangerous enemies of the German people.

IN FRANCE

The majority of the countries of western Europe

escaped an attack of the disease of antisemitism. In Scandinavia, Spain, Portugal, and Italy Jews were so few that they would scarcely have provided the minimum peg necessary for a political campaign based on their supposed iniquities or influence. In Great Britain the tremendous role played by Disraeli in national life as leader of the Conservative Party and prophet of the British Empire made the emergence of antisemitism as a political weapon inconceivable. There is, as a matter of fact, no evidence that the British at the time could have been persuaded that they were in any danger from their well-assimilated Jewish fellow-citizens. It is true that the Parliamentary battle to allow Jews to enter either House was long drawn out. But its length was not due to popular opposition or to public feeling, but to the innate conservatism of our institutions and to the dislike which even progressive-minded Englishmen feel towards the modification of any formula which has the sanction of long tradition—in this case the Parliamentary Oath of Allegiance taken "on the true faith of a Christian." It is more remarkable that antisemitism did not emerge into the political arena in either Holland or Belgium; for in the former country especially Jews were a prosperous and prominent community, and the relatively even division of the country between Roman Catholics and Protestants might have seemed to offer a favorable breeding ground for its use against one side or the other, especially in view of the part which the two churches played in the movement across the Rhine.

In France, however, there was a period of violent antisemitism at a moment when the main fires in Germany and Austria were dying down.

The Third French Republic came into existence after the defeat of Napoleon by Prussia in 1870. Military defeat was followed, especially in Paris, by a

19

period of revolutionary disorder which was suppressed with ruthless severity. The new government was nationalist, conservative, and not very republican; the influence of enemies of the republican form of government, whether monarchist or clerical, was strong in it, and it was only gradually that it assumed a more liberal and bourgeois appearance. But, once the monarchist element was defeated, the real battlefield emerged as a conflict between the clericals and the secularists, especially in the field of education. Napoleon III had encouraged religious control of education, and during his rule the church in France regained much of the ground which it had lost since the French Revolution. Many of the best schools were in the hands of the religious Orders, especially of the Jesuits. But the republican government was determined to obtain control of education, and to destroy the political influence of the church. The battle raged for many years, without a decisive victory on either side. But in 1892 a terrific financial scandal shook the stability of the republicans. The scandal was connected with the French Company interested in the digging of the Panama canal; and in the crash it was proved that many of the highest officials and most prominent politicians of the anti-clerical parties had been dangerously compromised, or even involved in extremely shady transactions.

There was at this time a highly organized and very vociferous antisemitic movement led by an able and unscrupulous demagogue, Edouard Drumont. The movement had extensive support in both military and clerical circles, but it had not yet actually launched itself into direct political action or directly challenged the republican form of government. It confined itself to agitation by meetings, by publications, and by its newspaper *La Libre Parole*. The situation in France was more difficult for the reactionaries than in Germany and Austria-Hungary. For the political influence of the old landed aristocracy had been almost completely eliminated by the Revolution of 1789. There was no group which still commanded a semi-feudal loyalty in the minds of the masses, and neither the Bourbon nor the Napoleonic claimants to the throne provided a good rallying ground. Even the church had not the basic authority it had in Austria. It enjoyed considerable political power, but it had had to struggle to obtain it, and knew it was insecure. But in 1894, while the republicans were still weakened by the Panama revelations, there seemed to be delivered into their hands the perfect opportunity for an onslaught on the republic, an onslaught in which the clerical and reactionary elements could make full use of the valuable weapon of antisemitism, while keeping their own monarchist and clerical pretensions in the background.

The General Staff had known for some time that there was a leakage of secret documents, in which some officer with access to confidential information must be involved; and in December a note was discovered giving a list of further documents which would be delivered to an attaché of the German Embassy. The note was declared by the staff officer in charge of the investigation to be in the handwriting of a certain Captain Alfred Dreyfus; and Dreyfus was an Alsation Jew. He was arrested and, in spite of his protestations of innocence, condemned to military degradation, and life imprisonment on Devil's Island. The fact of the condemnation of an officer for treason was published, but his name was not given until it was privately communicated by an officer concerned to Edouard Drumont, who immediately published that the traitor was a Jew. Certain details of the trial then leaked out, and caused some of the family of Dreyfus, as well as certain left-wing politicians, to doubt whether Dreyfus was really guilty or, at any rate, whether the trial had been fairly conducted. A certain disquiet made itself felt, and the antisemites seized their opportunity—the Jews and their allies were attacking the army!

This was a far better cause than the monarchy or the church for attracting immediate public sympathy. For the army occupied a peculiar place of affection in the hearts of all Frenchmen, who looked to it to avenge the dishonor of the disastrous defeat of 1870 and the loss of Alsace and Lorraine. The army was supposed to be above party politics, and its integrity, and the integrity of its leaders, were supposed to be above criticism and reproach. Therefore in casting doubts on the guilt of Dreyfus or on the fairness of his trial, 'the Jews and their allies' were impugning the honor of the army in a most tender spot, the integrity of military justice, and of the Ministry of War and the General Staff.

It is not necessary to recount in all its details the extraordinary story of the *affaire Dreyfus*. It is a story of forgery reinforced by forgery, of suicide and attempted judicial murder, of careers made and reputations broken, of extravagant coincidence and still more extravagant accusation. For five years French politics and social life were rent from top to bottom by the bitter feud between dreyfusard and anti-dreyfusard, and it was twelve years before the complete innocence of Captain Dreyfus was publicly admitted by both Chambers of the French Parliament and the Supreme Court of Appeal. But now after the days of France's tragic humiliation it is well to remember to her honor that a question of abstract justice and of the rights of a single obscure individual could so move to its depths the heart and mind of a great nation.

The clericals and anti-republicans had staked everything on the *affaire Dreyfus*, and the innocence of the Captain meant their complete downfall. Hence the bitterness with which they defended his guilt, and the trickery to which they descended to confute and over-throw his defenders. In their frantic maneuvers they compromised the army whose reputed integrity they had expected to use to compromise the government. So far from vindicating its honor, they caused the dis-grace and resignation of some of its highest officers. They compromised the church, for though it was only the clerical politicians who took open part in the affair, Roman Catholic sympathy was almost wholly on the side of the anti-dreyfusards. Above all they compro-mised the cause of religious education. Their fall brought about the complete separation of church and state, the complete control of education by the state, the exile of all the religious orders except those who consented to public registration and confined them-selves to work among the sick and poor, and, finally, the confiscation of church property. Apart from a brief period of mainly emotional influence immediately after the last war, the clericals disappeared from the re-mainder of the life of the Third Republic. They only regained the influence which they lost when they de-cided to make use of antisemitism, after the downfall of the Republic and the creation of Vichy France under Philippe Pétain.

In Russia

In western and central Europe the antisemitic parties betrayed their real intentions by the fact that they had no precise program for doing anything about the Jews. The formal cancellation of Jewish citizen-ship might, indeed, stand in their "Aims"; but they were far more concerned with general denunciations of the progressives than with any precise actions in the field of Jewish affairs. In Russia the situation was very different. There Jews were not citizens, and they were far more numerous than anywhere west of the Russian frontier. It had been the policy of the government for a long period to treat them with every kind of administrative hostility. In the period 1772-1812 Russia had acquired an enormous Jewish population—it finally amounted to about two-thirds of all the Jews of the world—by extending her frontiers to the west and south, and so absorbing the Jewish populations of ancient Poland, and of various territories bordering on the Black Sea.* In inner Russia Jews had never been allowed to dwell; and, with small exceptions, this rule held good until the end of Tsardom in 1917. In the 'Pale of Settlement' along the western borders of the country they were restricted both in their economic occupations and in their geographical distribution. The Russian Government did not know what to do about them; it wanted to convert them, but it feared to emancipate them or to give them complete social and economic rights. The Jews on the other hand did not easily accept suppression. Not only their native intelligence, but the cruel pressure of economic necessity, made them a perpetually restive element, and brought them into continually strained relations with many of their neighbors and with the authorities. There was no

*How Jews came to find themselves in these territories is part of the record of their history in the Middle Ages. They were largely the descendants of those who fled east and north out of the line of the Crusading armies of the 12th and 13th centuries, of those who fled from other persecutions during the later Middle Ages and of those who were attracted to the Kingdom of Poland by active kings who desired to encourage trade and industry among their subjects. The peasants were serfs; the nobility were too proud to engage in such activities. The Jews filled the gap. In the Crimea and southern Russia Jews had been settled since Roman times.

need to invent antisemitism in Russia. It existed already.

Further, in Tsarist Russia there was no Parliament and, in consequence, there were no defined progressive parties in the western European sense. But there were inevitably influential groups which had been affected by political developments in the west, and which desired to replace the Imperial autocracy resting on a vast nominated bureaucracy, by a constitutional monarchy resting on a Parliamentary régime. Although later many of the younger Jews were to be found among the various progressive groups, in the beginning, just because they lived such an isolated life, they played little part in these groups. To encourage the population to attack the Jews could, therefore, only at moments of extreme tension serve to render the general progressive movement unpopular. Such a moment occurred when Alexander II was assassinated in 1881.

At the beginning of his reign Alexander II had himself believed in a prudently progressive policy, and in 1861 he had achieved the complete emancipation of the millions of serfs who still formed the bulk of the peasants. But when it came to taking the next logical step, and to completing the value of personal liberty by the grant of political liberty, he and his administration drew back. The era of reforms came to an abrupt end, and the government settled down to its traditional autocratic policy. In such a situation it was inevitable that parties which in the west would be open and constitutional, should be secret and revolutionary. It was the members of one such secret group which in 1881, after several failures, succeeded in assassinating the Tsar.

His son and successor, Alexander III, hated all liberal and democratic ideas, and was determined to maintain the autocracy of his ancestors unimpaired. In this he had the full support of his bureaucracy, led by his old tutor, Constantine Petrovich Pobyedonostsev. They were determined to defend autocracy by every means in their power; but it did not help them to have to admit that there was such widespread and profound hatred of autocracy among the Tsar's own subjects that educated men and women were prepared to organize themselves secretly to assassinate their rulers. This was a moment in which, in imitation of the example of Germany and Austria, it was most useful to blame the Jews. Accordingly rumors circulated all through the south and west of the country, where the Jews lived, that it was the will of the Tsar that the murder of his father should be avenged on the Jewish people; and the ignorant peasants were given to understand that they had license to work their will (which turned to loot more than to massacre) during the Easter period. There is no doubt of the official inspiration of the pogroms which followed in many cities; the naive statements of peasants on trial betrayed it, even had other evidence been lacking; and, for the moment, it successfully deflected public attention from the underlying causes of the assassination.

During the next twenty years the administration continually harried its Jewish subjects, not only because it was the tradition of reactionary administrations so to do, but because it maintained the fiction that it was the Jewish element which was primarily responsible for the spread of liberal ideas in the Empire. In fact this was completely untrue; the centers of liberal and even revolutionary activity were to be found throughout the Russian universities—to which only the tiniest percentage of Jewish students were admitted—and in all Russian intellectual and professional circles—in which there were not half-a-dozen outstanding Jewish figures. But repression inevitably sent many young Jews into the rank and file of the revolutionaries, and a small group of them, of whom the chief was Leon Trotsky, joined the extreme revolutionary party, and shared their rise to power in October, 1917.

In 1894 Alexander III was succeeded by his son, the last Tsar, Nicholas II. Nicholas was, perhaps, of a mild and kindly disposition, but he was weak, obstinate and as determined as his father to preserve intact the autocratic government of his Empire against the demands of progress. In consequence his reign is a succession of defeats, of concessions made too meagerly and too late, culminating in 1917 in his abdication and his murder the following year. The peculiar feature of the antisemitism of the administration during his reign is that one of its main activities was to persuade the Tsar himself that his chief enemies were his Jewish subjects, that they were leagued against his person, his religion and his empire in a secret and determined world plot, and that only the most ruthless repression of the Jews would stamp out the liberal movement in the country.

A first step in the official propagation of this idea had been taken some decades previously, and it was possibly the fact that the same tactics had been employed for the 'education' of the bureaucracy and especially the political police, that suggested the subsequent fabrications (which became famous throughout the world as "The Protocols of the Elders of Zion") for the 'education' of the Emperor.

In the middle of the 1860's, Jacob Brafman, a Jewish 'convert' to orthodoxy who had turned police spy, offered 'evidence' to the reactionary Russian Governor of Vilna, Michael Muraviev, that there existed in the "Kahal"* a secret Jewish organization in Russia with widespread ramifications and despotic power over all Jewish communities. For a consideration he promised to reveal the secrets of the Kahal, and published a book which was based on the actual minutes of the officially recognized Jewish Kahal of Minsk fifty years previously. But, in the manner of Rohling in the west, these minutes, both innocent and dull in themselves, were embellished with faked Talmudic quotations and elaborate inventions by which the Kahal of Minsk was made to appear merely the local branch of a world Jewish Organization whose center was the recently founded philanthropic institution, the *Alliance Israélite Universelle*, of Paris. Brafman, however, achieved a triumph of which even Rohling did not dream. His *Book of the Kahal* was issued at the public expense and sent to all government officials as a guide in their relations with the Jewish population. It was particularly circulated among the political section of the police.

Fifteen years later another man of Brafman's calibre, but this time not of Jewish origin, came to add fuel to the fire. Hippolyte Lutostansky first appears as an ex-Roman Catholic priest in the middle-western province of Kovno, unfrocked by the Church authorities for a picturesque variety of offenses from embezzlement to rape. He then joined the Russian Orthodox Church, and became a student at a religious academy. Though entirely ignorant of Hebrew he selected as his subjects the ritual murder accusation and the Talmud. Having

---

*The word Kahal merely means community organization. Jews had possessed official "Kahals" until 1844 when they had been abolished and Jewish autonomy largely liquidated. It was the claim of Brafman that the organization had not disbanded, and had far wider influence than was known to the Russian authorities. For this he produced no evidence which stood the light of critical examination.

composed a scurrilous work on these subjects he tried to blackmail the Jewish community into paying for it not to be published. When this failed, he printed it, and had a copy accepted by the future Tsar Alexander III and by the chief of the political section of the police. This work also was circulated by the latter, at public expense, to all officers of his section throughout Russia.

When, therefore, at the beginning of his reign it seemed necessary to strengthen the conviction of the Tsar Nicholas II that the administration was really attacking the nerve center of liberal and revolutionary action in attacking the Jews, it is not surprising that the minds of the authorities should turn to the production of a new and fuller version of the work of Brafman and Lutostansky. Probably owing to the stress which had been laid on the supposed secret authority of the *Alliance Israélite Universelle,* the commission was entrusted to the Paris Office of the Russian police. And it was there that, between 1895 and 1900, the Protocols were fabricated. The story of their fabrication will be told in the next chapter, as a prelude to that of their distribution throughout the world. Here the Russian end of the story will be followed through. Almost every fact concerning their origin is veiled in mystery, including even the first date of their publication as a printed work. But this occurred somewhere between 1901 and 1905, a period of increasingly vehement demand for the granting of political rights.

As always happens when constitutional demands meet no response, power and influence had gone increasingly to the extremists, and the assassination of officials had become a daily occurrence. The Tsar's uncle, the Grand Duke Sergius, Governor of Moscow, many of the Tsar's Ministers, and thousands of the hated political police perished by the hand of revolutionaries, many of whom made no attempt to escape. Then in 1905 the Russians suffered a humiliating defeat at the hands of the Japanese, and, partly as a consequence of the loss of prestige following this defeat, and partly because of the steady increase of revolutionary violence, the Tsar in October issued a constitution and summoned a Parliament (Duma) for the following year. In the conflict between the Administration and both the revolutionaries and the elected representatives, which dragged on through the remaining years of the Empire, the former brought into being a pro-autocratic—Fascist as we would now say—organization called "the League of the Russian People," which replied with counter-violence alike to the violence of the assassins and the speeches of the constitutionalists. The pogroms against the Jews of 1905 and the following years were largely their work. The members of this patriotic League were often recruited from the hooligans of the slums, and were known as the "Black Hundreds." But the Tsar himself consented to be their patron and to wear their badge.

If the Tsar was prepared to go so far as to accept such an "honor," there was good reason to hope that the work produced by the Paris office of the police would be successful, and would bring about complete conviction in his mind as to the dangerous nature of Jewry. What happened to the document between 1900 and 1905 is unknown. Possibly the authorities who received it were themselves doubtful about its value; possibly it was mislaid, possibly—but why continue? Anything may have happened. But in 1905 it was finally issued to the public and presented to the Tsar. Strangely enough, it had very little effect on the Russian situation. The Tsar read the "Protocols," but in the end did not believe them to be genuine, and there is no evidence that copies circulated widely among the public, in spite of the book being re-issued several times.* The supreme effort of Russian antisemitism apparently fell flat. But once they were brought to western Europe, the story is very different. Since 1919 they have been issued in innumerable editions in many languages, and have been one of the main weapons of Nazi antisemitism throughout the world.

---

*It is for this reason that it is so difficult to-day to establish precise details of dates of publication; there are very few copies in existence inside or outside Russia. There is no mention of the Protocols in the standard work by Simon Dubnow on the Jews of Russia, published in 1916.

CHAPTER II

THE PROTOCOLS OF THE ELDERS OF ZION

JACOB BRAFMAN had pointed to the *Alliance Israélite Universelle* of Paris as the center of international Jewry; and the suggestion must have seemed reasonable to any Russian administrator who disliked the limelight which the Alliance was constantly throwing on the unhappy situation of the Jews in Russia; for it was foremost alike in asking for an amelioration of their lot and in helping the streams of unhappy refugees who were driven to seek refuge in western Europe or America. It was therefore in Paris that the political police determined to seek for further evidence of the sinister activities of Jewry, in order to convince the Tsar of the necessity of a policy of ruthless repression aginst his millions of Jewish subjects.

At the instruction of General Orgeyevsky, a leading official of the political police, members of that organization in Paris (where their task was to report on the activities of Russian emigrés and travellers) set to work to procure material. They were, however, not very competent historians, for the result of their labors entitled *The Mystery of Jewry,* was such a farrago of nonsense that when in 1895 General Orgeyevsky forwarded it to General Peter Alexandrovich Cherevin, Commander of the Imperial Guards, for communication to the Tsar, Cherevin decided to do nothing more than deposit it in the archives of the

political police. Here it was found and examined by
the Minister of the Interior, Peter Arkadyevich Stolypin (assassinated 1911), who wrote on it "this kind of
propaganda is wholly inadmissible to the government"
—which is not only a tribute to his intelligence, but
evidence that the intention of its creators and in-
spirers was that it *should* be used by the government,
as had been the works of Brafman and Lutostansky.

The Paris Office was then, presumably, instructed
to try again, and produce more satisfactory evidence.
The rest of the story, which is the story of the creation
of the Protocols, is completely shrouded in mystery,
up to the date of the first edition of which we have an
actual copy—the edition produced by Sergei Nilus and
printed in 1905. The difficulty is that all the editors
of the Protocols, while agreeing, of course, in asserting
that they are a genuine Jewish document, so totally
disagree as to how they came into existence that their
stories are of no value whatever in trying to trace the
document's history. But it seems most probable that,
under the supervision of General Rachkovsky, successor to General Orgeyevsky, they were fabricated in
the office which had just produced "The Mystery of
Jewry," and that they were then sent to the Headquar-
ters of the Police in St. Petersburg. This may have been
any time between 1895 and 1900. But, at first at any
rate, they shared the fate of their predecessor. They
failed to win acceptance, and they were not published.
But copies apparently circulated, for there is evidence
that various officials had them in their hands. Finally
through the instrumentality of a provincial 'Marshal
of Nobility' of the Province of Tver in southern Russia,
they came into the hands of a somewhat unstable and
excitable mystic, Sergei Nilus. Nilus translated them
into Russian from their original French and published
them under the melodramatic heading of *Antichrist:*

a near political possibility, as appendix to the second edition of a mystical work, *The Great in the Little*. Exactly what story was told to Nilus of their origin is obscure, though it is evident that he believed them to be absolutely genuine. But he gives no less than three separate and contradictory accounts of how they reached Russia, and one is left to conjecture. This much, however, is certain. He received them at a time when he was the center of a Court intrigue in which they were likely to be of considerable use to him. The superstitious susceptibilities of the Tsar and Tsarina, which were later revealed in their domination by Rasputin, manifested themselves from the beginning of their reign. In their early days a French adventurer, M. Philippe, was their favorite, and exercised considerable influence as a spiritualist and a Mason of a 'Martinist' lodge. The dowager Empress, and her sister-in-law, the Grand Duchess Elizabeth, wife of Sergius, the Governor of Moscow, were determined to find a strong and orthodox character to become confessor to the Tsar and to wean him from the sinister influences of M. Philippe. Their choice fell on Sergei Nilus whose mystical book had much impressed them. He was brought to Court, and instructed to prepare a new edition and present it to the Tsar. It is in this edition that the Protocols appear and, as on this first appearance Freemasons are named as jointly responsible with the Jews for a world plot again Christendom in general and Russia in particular, it is not too far-fetched to suppose that Nilus was provided with the document by the Dowager Empress, the Archduchess, or someone of their entourage, and that he was given a confused story of how they had been "discovered." For it was essential that he should believe them to be true. The reference to the Freemasons in this original version was, of course, directed against M. Philippe.

That the plot failed, and that Nilus never became confessor to the Tsar, is a side issue. The important fact is that through some connection with this plot the Protocols appeared. The book is not really a collection of "protocols" * at all, but rather a series of lectures supposed to be given by an "elder of Zion" to people to whom he could reveal with complete frankness the Jewish plot for which the Elders were responsible and the actual stage which they had at that moment reached. The many editors of the Protocols are as confused as to the identity of "the Elders of Zion" as they are on the subject of the origin of the document. They even differ as to the language in which the lectures were given.

On the background of a highly-colored but yet recognizable description of the troubles at the end of the 19th century, particularly in Russia—widespread unrest, a general breakdown of hitherto accepted standards of conduct, wars and acts of terrorism, growing national debts, and in the background the rising power of 'international finance'—the lecturer draws a picture of all these events as being the outcome of a deliberately conceived Jewish plot, which was manipulating national states and societies with the sole intention of securing the domination of Jewry. The industrious authors may have thought they were painting the portrait of a good revolutionary, but they certainly made him no stylist and a very poor thinker; for the lectures are verbose and tedious to a degree, and completely confused in their order. Moreover they have created the same confusion in the development

---

*According to the Oxford Dictionary the nearest meaning of *Protocol* would be "a formal or official statement of a transaction or proceeding."

of the plan of the plotters. In fact, though they are sufficiently alarming at first reading, it might be claimed that any plotters as muddled as the Elders could really only be a danger to themselves. At the same time, confused though they are, the story is unfolded with such a wealth of apparently convincing detail that it is easy to see that men might sincerely believe that 'there must be something in them' when they found one detail after another which appeared to them to give a possible interpretation of Jewish activities at the time; and it is this fact which gave the Protocols their tremendous vogue when they first came to western Europe and America at the end of the First World War.

It was a time when, for a brief moment, Jews seemed to be both prominent and powerful. By the Balfour Declaration the Zionists had secured a national Home in Palestine from the British Government in 1917; the first leaders of the Bolsheviks were all commonly believed to be Jews, and a certain number of them actually were; there had been Jewish leaders in the Communist *Putsches* in Germany and Hungary. But not only were the nationalist Jews and the revolutionary Jews apparently powerful, but ordinary Jewish citizens seemed more prominent than would be expected. There were British, French and American Jewish delegations at Versailles; President Wilson's most confidential adviser was an American Jew, and so on. Moreover men had been thrown off their balance by the strain of four years of war, and by the mass of confusing problems of which the new world seemed to be composed. There was confusion and disorder on all sides and men were prepared to believe what in more sober moments would have been rejected; the antisemitic movement of the previous thirty years had left memories. This passing prominence of the Jews reawoke them. The widespread reception of the Protocols as genuine is not really surprising in view of all these facts.

The *Morning Post* sounded the first cry of alarm in an article of August 7, 1917, which made the extraordinary statement that "the Jews are a great nation, emphatically a nation, and the *able statecraft of their secret rulers* has kept them a nation through forty centuries of the world's history. In their hands lies the traditional knowledge of the whole earth, and *there are no State secrets of any nation but are shared also by the secret rulers of Jewry.*"

In the turmoil and concentration of war the passage fell absolutely flat. The *Jewish Chronicle*, in a protest against the whole article, referred indeed to "insidious, not to say incoherent, incitements," but showed no special interest in the words I have italicized. The amazing statements that there had been a secret government in Israel since about 2000 B.C. (that is to say several centuries before Moses), that this government still existed, and that *there are no State secrets of any nation but are shared also by these secret rulers,* apparently aroused no comment.

In the following year (1918) the documents which were believed to prove these contentions, *The Protocols of the Elders of Zion,* were extensively hawked around the Ministries and newspaper offices of western Europe by White Russians. Extracts from them were simultaneously distributed to English and French officers serving in the White armies. Among the Russians in the same armies they had had a considerable effect, and the number of Jews who fell as victims to the fury of the soldiers of the anti-bolshevik forces in southern Russia ran into tens of thousands. But western Europe still refused to take them seriously.

At the end of 1919 the situation changed. In Novem-

ber a complete German translation was published,
and presented to the Princes of Europe in a dedication
which implored them to take heed while there was yet
time. In a lengthy introduction and a still longer clos-
ing comment the whole history of the Jews was reviewed, and their sinister influence on European history expounded—and it was emphasized that their tool
and partner in crime was unquestionably the British
Empire, and the vainglorious and arrogant British people. A couple of months later an English translation
appeared, which completely endorsed the German
view of the sinister rôle played by the Jews in European history, but naturally discovered the tool and
ally of Jewry not in England but in Germany. Almost
simultaneously lengthy extracts appeared in newspa-
pers in France and the United States, soon to be followed by complete translations of the documents. A
Polish edition was in existence in the beginning of
1920, and an Italian version followed later.

In February, 1920, the *Morning Post* reviewed the
English edition in a tone of serious alarm, recognizing
that the authenticity of the documents was not yet
proved, but expressing the belief that at least they
corresponded to the facts. In March a question was
asked in the House of Commons as to the advisability
of suppressing the documents on the ground that they
were a malicious attempt to stir up anti-Jewish feeling
and to injure the Entente. In May an anonymous correspondent in *The Times* drew attention to the fact
that no review of the documents had appeared in that
paper, and asking the agonizing question whether England had "by straining every fibre of our national body,
escaped a 'Pax Germanica' only to fall into a 'Pax
Judaica.'" In July, the *Morning Post* devoted seven-
teen special articles to the subject, and subsequently
republished them anonymously in book form, with an

alarmist introduction by the Editor himself, under the title of *The Cause of World Unrest*.

Finally, however, on August 11, 1921, the *Times* correspondent at Constantinople was able to produce conclusive evidence that they were a forgery. He obtained from a Russian refugee a coverless book which was subsequently identified as the *Dialogue aux Enfers entre Montesquieu et Machiavel*, and was, in fact, a satire on the ambitions of Napoleon III written by a French Radical lawyer, Maurice Joly (who was not a Jew). All that the authors of the Protocols had done was to substitute the "Elders of Zion" for Napoleon, and remake the material to suit their new purpose. Incidentally all strictures on the style and confusion of the Protocols fall on their authors, not on Joly. For the original is both brilliantly written and wittily conceived. The plot described by Joly is realistically and logically planned; it is the forgers who have hopelessly bungled the admirable original. But as proof of their dependence it may be said that, apart from hundreds of lines of adaptation and summary, over 180 passages, comprising 1,040 lines out of a total of 2,560 have been lifted bodily and without alteration, either of order or of content, from the *Dialogue*. In nine of the 24 Protocols more than half comes direct from Joly. Much of the addition was to dress the material for Russian consumption; and some of it can even be traced again to previous sources. The forgers were not very original!

What is interesting is to find that passages which do seem accurately to describe particular *Jewish* situations were taken bodily from Joly and actually describe the policy of Napoleon III, or what Joly thought the Emperor would like to do if he could.

Jews, for example, did own a good deal of the Central European press. Jewish journalists wrote a considerable proportion of its cultural and political articles; and the international news agencies of Reuter and Wolf were founded by Jews. It might then be thought to be established that the Protocols had a genuine Jewish origin, when we find in Protocols V and XII that:

> nowadays it is more important to disarm the peoples than to lead them into war: more important to use for our advantage the passions which have burst into flames than to quench their fire: more important to catch up and interpret the ideas of others than to eradicate them. The principal object of our directorate is this: to debilitate the public mind by criticism; to lead it away from serious reflections calculated to arouse resistance; to distract the forces of the mind towards a sham fight of empty eloquence. . . . In order to put public opinion in our own hands we must bring it into a state of bewilderment, by giving expression from all sides to so many contradictory opinions and for such length of time as will suffice to make the Goyim lose their heads in the labyrinth.

or again, that:

> not a single announcement will reach the public without our control. Even now this is already being attained by us inasmuch as all news items are received by a few agencies, in whose offices they are focused from all parts of the world. These agencies will then be already entirely ours and will give publicity only to what we dictate to them.

But in fact these passages are taken straight from the designs attributed to Napoleon III; that is, they are the opinions of Machiavelli in the *Dialogue*. In the seventh dialogue Machiavelli says:

> Today it is less a question of doing men violence than of disarming them; less of suppressing their political passions than of wiping them out; less of combating their instincts than of changing them by appropriating them to oneself. . . . The principal secret of government consists in enfeebling the public spirit to the point of disinteresting it entirely in the ideas and the principles with which revolutions are made nowadays. In all times people, like individuals, have been paid in words. . . . We must benumb (public opinion), strike it with uncertainty by astounding contradictions, work on it with incessant diversions, dazzle it with all sorts of different actions, mislead it imperceptibly in its pathways.

And in the eleventh he says:

> How does foreign news arrive? By a few agencies which centralize the news which is transmitted to them from the four quarters of the globe. Well, I suppose these agencies could be paid, and then they will give out no news except by order of the government.*

Moreover the relation of these passages to each other is exactly similar in both works. References which editors of the Protocols have found to 'international finance,' to the Bolshevik Revolution, and to other 'Jewish' activities, will similarly be found in almost

---

*The quotations from the Protocols are from the edition of *The Britons*, pp. 26 and 42: those from the *Dialogue* are from pp. 72 and 134 in the original, and from pp. 116 and 150 in the translation in *The Truth about the Protocols*, H. Bernstein, on which the above text is based.

41

identical language, and in the same sequence, in the *Dialogue.*

There is then no doubt that the content of the Protocols came from Joly. But the form was borrowed from a story which had already been printed on various occasions in Russia. The idea of "Elders of Zion" meeting secretly is found in a work of a German novelist, Herman Goedsche, who wrote thrillers in the 1860's and '70's under the romantic pseudonym of Sir John Retcliffe. In one of these, *To Sedan,* there is a chapter describing, with all the proper effects of a good thriller, a secret meeting in the ancient Jewish cemetery of Prague which is overheard by two strangers. Once every century the Elders of all the Tribes of Israel (Goedsche is a little shaky on his tribes) meet to plan their conquests for the succeeding century. The President is, of course, the Devil who appears and disappears with blue flames and in the form of a monstrous golden calf.

When doubts were first cast on the authenticity of the Protocols antisemitic parties responded by producing a number of other documents which, according to them, confirmed the reality of a Jewish plot. With all of them we cannot deal, but this secret meeting of the Elders at Prague is the basis of one of the most frequently quoted. It is, therefore, interesting to trace the record of this 'evidence' which first appeared as a piece of straight, sensational fiction—and as fiction it is fairly good, and worthy of a place in a "Century of Ghost Stories."

Not only do the two people in the novel who secretly overheard the meeting become real people who are pursued by the infuriated Elders (and are given various names), but Sir John Retcliffe, the nom-de-plume of Goedsche, passes through various transformations until he finally becomes John Readcliffe, chief rabbi of

London! In 1872 this particular chapter of the novel was republished in Russia as a novelette. It was still presented as fiction, but the sinister words were added that it *was not wholly the invention* of Sir John. In 1886 the story reappeared in France as the speech of a Grand Rabbi, made in 1880 and "extracted from an advance copy of the forthcoming work of the distinguished English diplomat, Sir John Readcliff, entitled *Annals of the politico-historical events of the last ten years.* It was next published in a Russian newspaper in Odessa as the speech of a rabbi made to the secret sanhedrin of 1869 (apparently a reference to the First Congress of Reform Judaism which was held in that year at Leipzig). The Russian was translated from the French translation of the English translation of the original Hebrew, and its authenticity was fully vouched for by the fact that it was published by Sir John Readcliff, an aristocrat of the notoriously Judeophil country, England.

But when the non-existent Readcliff, or Retcliffe, had finally fallen a victim to the Elders, as several authors assure us was the case, the speech continued to be reported. The antisemitic *Deutsch-soziale Blätter* reported an unnamed rabbi as having made it in 1893. It was next reported as having been made at a non-existent Zionist Congress at Lemberg in 1912, and by this time the orator is called either Reichorn or Eichorn. Finally, in 1921, after the exposure of the forgery of the Protocols, it was brought out again, on the basis of the Odessa text of 1882.

In one form or another it is to be found in almost any antisemitic collection of documents; and having acquired a good deal of variety in its migrations, different texts are then used to bolster up each other's authenticity. But in fact they betray themselves in an odd and unexpected fashion. At the original meeting of the

Elders at Prague Goedsche gives a list of all the stock-exchanges which are supposed to be in the hands of the Jews, and this list occurs *in exactly the same order* in all the versions. But "Paris, London, Vienna, Berlin, Amsterdam, Hamburg, Rome and Naples" is not so inevitable an order that its constant recurrence does not prove one common source for all the speeches. Moreover while the stock exchange of Naples may have had some importance before the unification of Italy in 1870, it had little afterwards, and yet it is still quoted in versions of the speech supposed to have been given long after that date.

It would be tedious to recount all the other documents used by antisemitic parties. They are alike in their inability to stand the test of critical examination. And most of them, by their naiveté, betray the class of the community to which they expect to make an appeal. One antisemitic writer, whose pseudonym is Ernest Sincere, reaches the height of absurdity when he states that this supposed Jewish plot was started in 929 B.C. by King Solomon, and is carried on by the Elders of Zion with the assistance of exactly one million nine hundred and twenty-one thousand, six hundred and one fellow-plotters. We are thus presented with a secret shared by 1,921,601 people which has been in existence 2,874 years, and is still not susceptible of any real proof! Really if 1,921,601 people can keep a secret for 2,874 years they deserve to succeed!

CHAPTER III

GERMANY OF THE NAZIS

THE advantage which could be gained by diverting public attention to the Jews was clear to the enemies of the German Republic of 1919. It was at one time fashionable to ascribe almost all the evil elements in the Germany of 1919-1939 to the effects of the hostility of the victorious allies and the severity of the Treaty of Versailles; and it would appear to be true that there was a period in the middle twenties when a different policy and a determined effort at reconciliation might well have proved successful. But even at this period there would have been no universal abandonment of the dream of revenge, or universal acceptance even of a share of the guilt of the war. From the beginning there were strong groups in Germany which regretted not the war, but only the defeat, and desired to regain the lost influence of Germany as a great power only that she might become powerful enough to seek revenge. As the years went on the weaknesses and mistakes of successive republican governments steadily increased the influence of these groups, and it was among them that Hitler found his followers, and out of their feelings that he built up his political propaganda.

Everything which Germans resented or regretted was most skillfully attributed to the Republic, always called by the Nazis "the System," a vague all-embracing word, covering social and moral issues as well as political. Still, something more concrete was also necessary; but it had not only to be concrete but also to be safe. Germany was far too weak in the early days of the Nazi movement for public attention to be directed at the real enemies, France, or the Allied Powers in general; and the Nazi Party within Germany was also too weak to risk carrying its attack against the Government to the point of compelling them to take really vigorous action. Nor could even "the System" be usefully made the sole menace, so long as there was little hope of destroying it by frontal attack. What was wanted was an enemy sufficiently concrete to be usable in the most vulgar propaganda addressed to the most ignorant sections of the populace, and sufficiently weak to give the Nazis a cheap victory, both psychological and physical. The Jews of Germany exactly fitted the picture.

They were only one per cent of the population; and the relics of the antisemitism of the 19th century, together with the effects of the constant insistence on the Protocols and the 'Bolshevik menace,' ensured that they would find no very valiant defenders. The Republicans, already on the defensive themselves, were not likely to endanger their popularity still further by defending the Jews. There was also this extra advantage. As in other countries, so in Germany, their history has caused the Jews to be concentrated both geographically and occupationally. They could easily be made to appear much more prominent (and therefore, from the standpoint of Hitler's propaganda, much more dangerous) than they really were. With such skill and with such constant reiteration were the different misrepresentations driven home that they came to be widely believed to be true, not only in Germany itself, but wherever Nazi influence penetrated in other

46

countries. There are many people in this country who believe that before 1933 Germany was "dominated by the Jews," so assiduously was this 'fact,' supported with well-selected statistics, pumped into every visitor to the Reich. Jews were certainly prominent in the cultural and professional life of Berlin, and in certain sections of its business life. Berlin statistics would therefore be given as though they covered the whole country; similarly the statistics of the particular aspect of a trade or profession in which Jews were numerous were given as though they represented the Jewish proportion in the whole trade or profession. And the word 'dominant' was so constantly used as a complete synonym for 'prominent' that men actually came to believe that it was only necessary to show that 10 per cent of an occupation was in Jewish hands, for this profession to be 'dominated' by the Jews. To the Nazis, of course, the Weimar Republic and the Weimar parliament were both entirely controlled by the Jews. How, they did not trouble to state.

A second story which was widely circulated was that Germany had been inundated with 'foreign Jews' during the period of inflation. Germany has always had excellent official statistics, and in actual fact this flood amounted to less than one for every thousand of the population, and the majority of these were poor Jews who had fled from the unsettled conditions of Poland and eastern Europe. But a third story attributed to this element all the scandals of the inflation period, and asserted that they had made great fortunes out of the German people, and then flaunted them in the face of the national poverty. It was certainly true of some individual cases, and one or two of the really bad scandals of this period did involve individuals among these 'foreign' Jews. But the real profiteers of the inflation were the great industrialists and the landowners. Some

47

were able to pay off their debts and mortgages, con-
tracted in pre-1914 marks when they stood at 20 to the
£ sterling, when the mark had fallen to one thousand
millionth of its value. Others, especially Hugo Stinnes
(who was not a Jew), by an ingenious system of bor-
rowing from the State Bank and repaying the loan
when the mark had fallen heavily, were able to buy
up industries in every field and make enormous profits.

Different arguments against the Jews were addressed to different classes of the population among
whom Hitler hoped from the first to win supporters.
By pretending that he would cleanse the professional
life of the country of Jewish elements, he held out the
possibility of work to the thousands of graduates of
the universities, technical and secondary schools who
were constantly unemployed; and these unemployed
youths formed a considerable proportion of his early
storm troopers. By 'fighting against the influence of
foreign elements,' he appealed to the Nationalists; and
by concentrating exclusive attention on Jews as the
profiteers from the inflation, he provided a comfortable
smoke-screen for the industrialists and landowners,
while at the same time continuing to pose as a friend
of the German working men. How effective this policy was is shown by the enormous contributions heavy
industry, and capitalists generally, made to his funds.

But the Jews were used not merely for these concrete purposes; they had to be found a place in the
inevitable background of any political movement in
Germany—its *Weltanschauung*, or philosophy of life.
Race and soil were the foundation ideas of Hitler's
Weltanschauung, and the Jews were to him the racial
poison of the world, just as the Aryan was the racial
hero. Racial antisemitism had made its first appearance in the middle of the 19th century. A French political philosopher, De Gobineau, had introduced it, and

a much greater French scholar, Ernest Renan, had, in his earlier years especially, written much against the 'semitic spirit.' But the full antithesis Aryan-Semite was finally brought out by a curiously fascinating writer, a German citizen of English birth, Houston Stewart Chamberlain. In a work filled with perverted erudition, entitled *The Foundations of the 19th Century*, published in 1899, he traced the conflict of the Aryan and the Semitic spirit all through history. His method of deciding what was Aryan was simple. Everything which in his judgment was noble in history was Aryan, and no further proof was needed than that he was an Aryan himself and felt the kinship in his blood. As Chamberlain was one among many who were fascinated by the racial idea, and as it was not to be expected that the likes and dislikes of all members of that school would be identical, the results of this simple method of proving what was Aryan were often amusing. Thus to Chamberlain himself Goethe was so perfect an example of the purest Aryan that he quoted him in his *Foundations* no less than 127 times (according to the index). But another writer of the same school, Lenz, calls Goethe a "Teutonic-Western-Asiatic crossbreed," and proves it by an examination of the poet's mentality; while yet a third, Otto Hauser, proves his mongrel nature by the fact that in *Faust* there are "hundreds of quite pitifully bad verses." Later, in Nazi days, the same division arose about Christianity and Christ himself; to the German Christians, Christ was an Aryan;* but to the neo-pagan of the Rosenberg school, Christianity was the typical semitic, un-aryan teaching which could only under-

---

*I remember a Nazi theological student being very surprised that I, as a theologian, had not been taught that Jesus was a German, son of a German soldier and a Persian woman. He appeared, quite sincerely, to believe that this was an accepted conclusion of scholarship.

mine the proud Aryan spirit by its inculcation of a slave mentality. Hitler himself read Chamberlain with avidity, and found in him authority for his own dreams. They gave the apparatus of 'scholarly' profundity to the views which he had adopted from his teacher and idol, Lueger, the antisemitic Mayor of Vienna. When, therefore, the National Socialist German Workers' Party came into existence, it was laid down that only those of German blood could be German citizens.

Although Hitler almost certainly believed passionately in the truth of his views about the Jews, he never made any secret of the fact that antisemitism was also a most useful weapon in every field of his propaganda;* and when the Nazis came into power in 1933, it was systematically infiltrated into every department of life from mathematics and religion to children's books and pornography; and broadcast, as an integral part of the Nazi way of life, from every diplomatic and consular office abroad. The German mind desires things to be both orderly and solid—*grundlich*. The statements made in the propaganda of the previous ten years had to be seriously embodied in every aspect of public, national life. Scientists, historians, philosophers, jurists were all set to the task of proving in their respective subjects that it was incontrovertibly true that the Jews were such as Hitler and others had described them, and that there could be no doubt about it.

The main difficulty was, of course, to say what *was*

---

*"Antisemitism is a useful revolutionary expedient. Antisemitic propaganda in all countries is an almost indispensable medium for the extension of our political campaign. You will see how little time we shall need in order to upset the ideas and criteria of the whole world, simply and purely by attacking Judaism. It is beyond question the most important weapon in my propaganda arsenal."

Adolf Hitler, quoted by H. Rauschning.

a Jew, and, fantastic as it may seem when one regards the immense superstructure built upon the thesis of the danger of the 'Jewish poison,' that problem always defied solution. At one time it was proudly announced that a scientist had elaborated an instrument—apparently rather like a metronome—whose pendulum revolved in dignified and rhythmic ellipses when in the presence of Aryan blood, but in short and erratic jerks at the proximity of a Jew; at another time some particular physical feature or organ was proclaimed to yield decisive and objective evidence to scientific examination. I am told that wounded Nazis have been known to prefer death to a blood transfusion from blood which was, or might be, Jewish, in the firm belief that 'Jewish blood' would poison them. But all efforts were in vain. It was never possible to go beyond the statement originally made that a Jew was a person whose grandparents were of the Jewish religion. Certain classes, Nazi officials, and those entitled to a hereditary peasant holding, had to go beyond their grandparents, and produce 'aryan' ancestry back to the year 1800; but even then, if a doubtful ancestor occurred, the only test could be: were his or her grandparents Jews? The result was an army of officials to search and check registers, frenzied questions addressed to officials of all types in all parts of the world, and, no doubt, a good deal of graft to provide satisfactory pedigrees. But it remained obstinately true that it was impossible scientifically to establish what exactly it was to be a Jew.

This, however, was almost the only flaw in a system which was monumentally complete in its perversity. An institute in Berlin and another in Munich produced ponderous and apparently scholarly tomes on the place of the Jews in German history. They were written by men familiar with the technique of research and, with

51

their mass of references, quotations and footnotes, were quite capable of passing as genuine and objective historical studies. In every university, and on every faculty, were appointed professors who—in spite of the basic difficulty of deciding what or who was a Jew—were quite capable of delivering lectures to distinguish the German and the Jewish spirit in law, in medicine, in philosophy, in art, in psychology and even in mathematics. Naturally the outside world perceived a considerable falling off in the merits of German scholarship, but this did not influence the Nazis, who only saw in the contempt of the academic world abroad further evidence of the power of the pernicious influence of Jews throughout the world. A new Protestant Church came into existence which would not accept Jewish converts, and which stripped the Christian religion and the Christian scriptures of their 'Jewish perversions.' The Nazis did not stop at educating the new generation, vitally important though this was to their success. By lectures, by the use of all the professional and scientific publications with which Germany abounded, and by the strictest and most careful control of all the professional, commercial and other associations, the Nazi view on race was inculcated into the whole middle class with a thoroughness, and an apparent irrefutability, which was bound to have a profound effect on the actual thinking and beliefs of the victims. Apparently sober and factual statements, balanced by statistics, were handed out to visitors. In consequence many who visited Germany in the years between 1933 and 1939, and who had known the previous situation, reported that so far as the Jews were concerned the Nazi view was extremely widely accepted.

But with the general public other methods were used, and every kind of violence and vulgarity was not only permitted but definitely encouraged. The bullying of Jews, adults or children, was considered to be of great value in teaching German youth to despise sentimental pacifism, internationalism, or Christian morality. A picture book which was issued by the *Stürmer* for children, and which was written and illustrated by a girl in her teens, begins with the good medieval statement that the father of the Jews is the devil, and continues, with illustrations which would give an English child nightmares if its foolish parents allowed it to read it, to present the Jews as obscene and disgusting polluters of German blood and life. Throughout it seeks to inculcate into the youngest the idea that it is noble to fight against the Jewish people including, of course, their children. Schoolmasters reinforced the lesson by publicly insulting Jewish children in their classes, and repressing all signs of tenderness or sympathy on the part of other children. Some of the effects of this work among the young are told, with impressive restraint, by Amy Buller in her recent book *Darkness over Germany*. Even those whose chosen reading was pornography were given a satisfying weekly diet of rapes, assaults and what-not by Julius Streicher, one of Hitler's closest friends, in *Der Stürmer*.

Antisemitism was thus woven into every strand of the thought and action of Hitler's Germany; it was also inextricably interwoven into her economic policy. The considerable sums of capital extracted from her half-million Jews formed an invaluable fund for the manipulations of Dr. Schacht; confiscation offered endless possibilities of blackmail not only to individual Nazi officials, but to the German government in its foreign commercial relations. And, of course, it provided a quantity of houses, furniture, *objets d'art*, and jobs to Hitler's followers. Not even in Tsarist Russia was antisemitism so intimately interwoven into the whole life of a people. There were, of course, a minority who saw through it, and who rejected all its premises; but the tragic evidence is that the bulk of the German people were sufficiently hypnotized by the pseudo-scientific and statistical justifications of the government and every public speaker to accept with no more than a regretful shrug the violences, indecencies, murders and suicides which accompanied them. They were convinced that Jewry was a vast and hostile world force, destroying and disintegrating all they held sacred, an enemy so powerful that all means were justified in the defense of their 'aryan' culture and nation.

Result—the bestial cruelty thousands of Germans inflicted on Jews in death camps and torture chambers.

The propaganda which had so effectively created this picture within Germany did not stop at the German frontier. Antisemitism was Germany's most valuable *exportartikel*. The world will never know how many billions of dollars were officially spent by Nazi Germany in financing antisemitic propaganda, in England, in France, in Belgium and Holland, in Hungary, Poland and Rumania, in South Africa, in Canada, in the United States and in the whole of South America. The same technique was applied as at home. There would be more or less restrained and apparently quite objective statistics; organizations would be fostered, such as the Anglo-German Fellowship, and the Link, which apparently only desired closer friendship in the interests of peace; antisemitic propaganda would be presented in a reasonable, almost regretful, tone. It would be suggested that of course these measures in Germany had only been necessary because the German situation was *different;* Germany had a different type of Jew; and so on and so on. And fascists in other countries assisted by saying the same thing from their own point of view. An excellent example of this stage is provided by the British Union of Fascists. In a signed statement contributed by Sir Oswald Mosley to *The Jewish Economic Forum* on July 28, 1933, he makes the following declaration:

"The British Union of Fascists is not anti-Semitic.

Attacks on Jews in any shape or form were strictly forbidden within a month after the movement was launched.

This order has been loyally obeyed by all the members.

The few who did not agree to do so were excluded from the movement.

Fascism stands for religious and racial tolerance.

If a Jew is associated with Communism or the financial policy which we are up against, we shall fight him not as a Jew but as an opponent.

We have no quarrel with Jews as Jews, just as we have no quarrel with Catholics as Catholics.

Fascism is in no sense anti-Semitic, and bias for or against the Jews is completely irrelevant to the issues involved in our political creed.

Anti-Semitism was never known in Fascist Italy, and Mussolini has often expressed himself in this sense.

The attacks on the Jews in Germany do not rest on any Fascist principle but are the manifestation of an inherent quality in the German character.

This issue has always arisen in Germany in one form or another in times of crisis.

It is foolish to blame Fascism for something that has its source in the mentality of a particular nation, or at least of a considerable section of that nation.

Here in Great Britain Fascism is British through and through. It is backed by the national character, which has never countenanced and always opposed religious and racial persecution.

For many centuries religious and racial tolerance has been part of the British character, and I give my assurance that under Fascism that great tradition will be preserved."

At the top of the Declaration is, appropriately enough, a photo of Mosley beside Mussolini at a Fascist parade. But not many years had passed before Mosley, after a visit to Germany, was doing his best to attract the attention he had thus far failed to obtain, by stirring up antisemitism in the poorer quarters of the East End of London, where many thousands of Jews lived. Whether Mosley received subsidies from the Nazis or not has never been established; but this much is certain, that he made full use of Nazi material provided for him on the Jewish question.

This provision of material for local use proved an invaluable line of attack. Several institutes in Germany, generously provided with funds, were churning out continuously, and in many languages, all the usual Nazi material on the Jews. The same stock quotations, or misquotations, occur in apparently quite independent publications in Montreal or Buenos Aires, in Brussels or Bucharest. And in every language edition after edition of the Protocols was issued and circulated. On several occasions these editions of the Protocols were the subject of trials for defamation, but it made no difference to the Nazi antisemitic campaign. If a line of attack was blocked in one place, it was easy to open it in another. If one quotation was discredited, another could easily be substituted. But usually they did not trouble. In the world, discontent and frustration of the thirties, they had no need to worry about their failures.

Much of this material was actually printed in Germany, and distributed through the German communities living abroad. These, in their turn, formed valuable centers for the dissemination of antisemitism. In England it was discreetly done at private meetings and dinner parties, and it was largely the 'upper' classes which were thus infected. In South Africa the activities of the German community in the previously German colony of South-West Africa compelled the South African Government to take serious steps against them. In South America, and to a lesser extent in the U.S.A., the local German Nazis, supported by the German diplomatic and consular representatives, largely succeeded in terrorizing the non-Nazi German population into acquiescence and even support of their activities.

In many countries it was possible to go still further. In some, as in England, there already existed obscure fascist bodies; in others, such as Poland and Rumania, full-blown antisemitic organizations had already been in existence for some time. In both cases these parties were more closely linked with Germany. Their leaders were invited to Berlin, and there flattered and advised how to extend their influence; it was after one such visit that Mosley suddenly changed over from his previous attitude and flung himself into the vulgarest antisemitism on the straight Nazi model. These apparently patriotic parties were used to forward definite German ambitions, and to demand the orientation of national policy in a pro-German sense, with complete disregard for the real national interests of the countries in which they existed. This was conspicuous in Poland in the period before 1939 in which she was quitting the orbit of French influence and entering into close friendship with Germany. In Hungary and Rumania German policy was equally selfish. In every case there

was one common feature. Germany would not nego-
tiate with, or support, a group which did not adopt
her antisemitic policy. In 1933, when Hitler had only
just come to power and Mussolini was definitely the
senior partner of the Fascist firm, Mosley could write:
"Antisemitism was never known in Fascist Italy, and
Mussolini had often expressed himself in this sense."
But gradually the balance of power shifted. As Hitler
consolidated his government, the greater wealth and
population of Germany, together with the drain caused
by the Abyssinian adventure of Mussolini, enabled
Hitler to demand that his partner should also toe the
line. Mussolini was compelled to eat his words and
make the discovery that the Jews were a sinister force;
he was obliged to forget that there were Jews among
his oldest collaborators, and, much more important,
that there were distinguished Jews in all the professions and public services of Italy who had never known
the slightest distinction between themselves and other
Italians. In fact neither they themselves, nor the rest
of the Italian population, were easily able to discover
who were members of the Jewish community and who
were not, so completely had their small numbers been
integrated into Italian life. But the familiar rhythm was
forced into operation. First it was the 'foreign' Jews—
many of them exiles from Germany who had been invited to Italy—who were found to be a menace; then
the attack was made on Italian-born Jews, on the German model. All that can be said in Italy's favor is that
it was not made with quite the German brutality.

In several countries of eastern Europe the policy
was necessarily somewhat different. Polish or Hungarian antisemites did not need literary assistance, or instruction about 'the menace of the Jews.' In fact there
were real problems, such as had never existed in Germany, connected with the position of the Jews in cer-

tain of these countries. Here Nazi policy was to support these groups openly against their governments;
to publicize as 'martyrdom' any measures which
governments might take against them; and so to ensure that they should naturally look to Germany for
support, if and when there was a chance of their attain-
ing power. The brief fascist government of Rumania in
1937-8 acted entirely in accordance with Nazi wishes.

But before 1939 Nazi Germany did not reveal the
full import of her contacts with these national organizations in which she had planted and tended so assiduously the seeds of antisemitism. Their full scope the
world only discovered in 1940. Quisling in Norway,
Mussert in Holland, Degrelle in Belgium, the Cagoulards and similar groups in France—all had been the
spearheads of the antisemitic movements in their
countries; all of them were distinguished from other
extreme Nationalist movements—such as the Flemish
movement in Belgium—by the fact that when the crisis
came they willingly acted as traitors in the German
interest.

In the pre-war years Germany had yet one further
poisoned shaft for spreading the virus of her antisemitism—her own Jewish citizens. From 1933 onwards, but particularly in the year or two immediately
preceding the war, Jewish refugees from Germany
were unscrupulously exploited, even after they had
been robbed of both property and home. In this exploitation the national fascist parties, in particular the
British Union of Fascists and the fascist organizations
in the United States, such as those of Father Coughlin
or Pelley, took a prominent part. The world was bare-
ly recovering from the immense depression of the
early thirties. In every country the working and professional classes were, by and large, convinced that the
admission of immigrants meant the reduction of the

number of jobs available for natives; there was no great difficulty in stirring up opinion against any additions to the population. Some of the refugees arrived looking very prosperous. The reason was that, as they were allowed to take so little of their cash out of the country, the sensible thing was to buy as many clothes, as much furniture, as possible. It not only avoided further purchases, but might, if necessary, be sold. But the antisemitic parties were there to shout that they showed no sign of ill-usage or of misery, and that many native workers would be glad to be as well clad as these "so-called refugees." Others arrived penniless; and these were easy game for the allies of the Nazis, who proclaimed that they had clearly come to take their jobs from Englishmen, from Frenchmen, from Americans, Canadians—whoever it might be. All round the world the same technique, the identical methods of attack, betrayed the same master hand, the same center of instructions.

Finally there was the Arab world. This was selected for special care and attention. Prominent Nazi leaders took 'holidays' in Arab countries. Considerable numbers of Arab students were given scholarships to study in Germany, or at least free travel to visit Nazi conferences and meetings. While Mussolini poured out from his radio station at Bari anti-British anti-Jewish broadcasts, the Nazi, with great thoroughness, fished in the troubled waters of the Middle East, harping always on the two themes of the iniquity of the British and the iniquity of the Jews. There is nothing surprising in the Mufti finding a final home in Berlin; or in the rising in Iraq in 1941. Both were the result of years of careful German preparation.

Of any concerted Jewish world plot there is no evidence whatever. The international Jewish organizations, such as they are, are weak, divided, and perpetually hampered for funds. But an *anti*-Jewish world plot existed openly in the years from 1933 to 1939. It was backed by the whole network of Nazi diplomatic agencies throughout the world. It took litle note of customary diplomatic behavior; it had no scruples about interfering in the life and internal affairs of other countries. It included blackmail and assassination in its armory. It was possessed of limitless funds, much of them stolen from Jewish citizens of Germany. It has made the whole world Jew-conscious; it has deluged it with such masses of propaganda, such skilfully falsified statistics, such cunningly perverted regrets and explanations, that it is not surprising that much of it has found a home in the most innocent minds, and has left a heritage which will bear evil fruit for a long time, even though Hitler himself and his colleagues have been overthrown.

CHAPTER IV

THE OTHER SIDE OF THE PICTURE

DIFFICULT as it may be to believe, this immense anti-semitic movement, which for sixty years has disturbed the political life of the world, and has culminated in the deliberate and cold-blooded murder of more than four million men, women and children, has only the most tenuous connection with any reality of past or present Jewish history.

There is nothing obscure about the history of the Jews in the 19th century; nothing obscure about the jealousies they created here, the enmities they aroused there; their failures and successes, their wealth and poverty; their inner struggles and conflicts. It is only to the antisemites that Jewish history is full of sinister and inexplicable mystery.

If their story is to be understood, the first essential is that their 19th century history should be grafted on to the experiences of their long exile. For it is in the exile that they became an abnormal people. That is not to say that before it they were universally beloved, and were never a problem to anyone. That would not be the true story of any of the peoples who inhabit this globe. But in the days of Egypt, Greece and Rome, when Jews were disliked they were either disliked for something they had actually done, or because of some explanation (which, indeed, may well have been inaccurate) of some real trait in their character or feature in their situation. Roman society, for example, was tolerant of all religions. But Jewish worship of one God naturally involved the rejection of the religions of other people. This rejection was *explained* as being due to their "hatred of the human race." The explanation was inaccurate, but it is not surprising that it made the Jews unpopular; especially as it did apparently explain something which could easily be observed as an unusual trait by any one in contact with the Jews—that they would not eat with Gentiles, for example. Such things are part of the normal life of imperfect men and imperfect societies on this imperfect planet.

It was anti-Jewishness, it was sometimes anti-Judaism; it wasn't what to-day we call antisemitism. For the particular hallmark of antisemitism is that it can *not* be explained by the contemporary life or character of the Jews. The Jews have certain characteristics: but the antisemites invent quite different ones; Jews create certain problems: but not the problems the antisemite proclaims. True, one observable fact is needed, but only as a peg; and on that single peg the antisemite hangs not explanations but the most elaborate inventions.

The first fact in this drama of artificiality is religious. It was the fact that the Jews had not accepted Christianity. But as everyone knew—so ran the argument in early theological writers—that Christianity was true, the Jew was deliberately wicked in his rejection of it. The Old Testament was combed to find proof of his continual wickedness; and as the Old Testament contains the frankest national history that the historians of any nation have ever written, ample evidence was produced that they always had been "stiff-necked" and "perverse." It was easily 'proved' that they were stained with every hideous crime; that they revelled in wickedness. The explanation was clear; they were the self-chosen servants of the devil.

In the Middle Ages this was taken as proved. The Jews were less than human; they waited for the coming of the anti-Christ; and in the meanwhile the devil employed them to do all they could to harm the Christian cause and Christian nations. They mixed magic potions to poison them—so the Middle Ages explained the Black Death which destroyed a third of the population of Europe in 1348 and the following years—and their practice of medicine only covered their designs on Christian lives; they insulted the Christian religion, spitting on and defiling its sacred statues and objects of cult, mocking it and blaspheming against it in their evil books; dark stories circulated that they conspired with its enemies—human as well as Satanic—to blot it out; above all medieval man believed that they used Christian blood for their nefarious practices, and to cure themselves of the revolting smell and disgusting diseases which were the penalty of their unbelief; and that they constantly murdered children to secure the needed blood. And they were usurers, delighting to entangle Christians in their toils.

Here was the second *fact* in this farrago of nonsense. Many Jews *were* usurers: of course not all Jews practiced usury—nor did all Christians abstain from it. The statement that one constantly meets that "all usurers were Jews, because the church forbad usury" is as true as that all adulters were Mohammedans because the church forbad adultery. Still, sufficient numbers of Jews really were usurers for it to be an observable fact. The real reason has nothing to do with particular Jewish aptitudes. It lay in the political status of the Jews, their entire absence of freedom, and their complete ownership by the prince in whose territories they lived. The royal method of collecting a substantial proportion of their revenue was to license their Jewish serfs to lend money to their Christian subjects, and then collect the profits.

It was some centuries before a third fact could be added. It is wrong to stress, during the medieval period, the significance of the Jews as foreigners. Certainly their lack of a home of their own had a gradual effect on their own psychology, but medieval Europe was little conscious of differences of nationality, as those differences are understood today. Wars were dynastic, not national, and pieces of territory constantly changed hands with the marriages, defeats or victories of princes. A medieval noble would hold land in many different countries without any feeling of oddity on the part either of himself or of his tenants.

As Europe began to be conscious of national differences, this consciousness began to be doubly marked in the case of the Jews in their midst, because the 17th and 18th centuries are in some senses the 'dark ages' of Jewish history. Broken and embittered by centuries of persecution, poverty-stricken, and dealing only in the smallest and most ignoble trades, the appearance of the majority of the Jews in the 17th and 18th century was more distinctly and visibly 'foreign,' even if they rarely wore a badge, than it was in the Middle Ages.

To the third fact of *foreign-ness* was quickly added a fourth. With the French Revolution and the 19th century Jews began to become citizens of various countries of western Europe. In England, though legally and politically their rights were restricted until 1858, they enjoyed complete social freedom, and their communities were to be found in most of the cities, especially the sea-ports, of the country.

The fourth fact was the combination: *foreign-ness* + *citizenship.* On it, with a suitable rechauffée of all the previous fables, the immense structure of modern antisemitism was reared. This is not to say that there were not actual problems, both internal to the Jewish community, and arising out of Jewish-Gentile relationships, during the period. There were such problems, and some of them presented very real difficulties, but the antisemites required a larger canvas for their fantasies, and it is rare to find any serious study of actualities in antisemitic literature.

From the Jewish standpoint, the period from the French Revolution to the first World War was sharply divided into two by the events of the year 1881. In that year the Tsar, Alexander II, was assassinated, and the great exodus of Jews from Tsarist Russia began. More than a quarter of the whole Jewish population of the world was uprooted, not only from their country but even, one can say, from their century in the years between 1881 and 1914; and western Jewries doubled, quadrupled or more, at the influx of the Russian refugees.

In the early period two main problems confronted the Jewries of western Europe: the acquisition and the exercise of the rights of citizenship, and the absorption of the new knowledge and culture which their re-entry into European society made accessible to them. It was a dual problem of assimilation. The most devastating blow struck at Jewry by the Christian church had been the deprivation of citizenship. In the Roman Empire in New Testament times individual Jews could obtain citizenship. Later, citizenship was extended to all the population of the Empire, including Jews. From the beginning of the third century A.D. no political bar distinguished them from their neighbors, but even before they had always been free to follow, and had followed, all the occupations of the time. In the fifth century exclusion from citizenship in the Christian Roman Empire began as religious intolerance, but soon led to both social and economic consequences. The narrowing of the range of Jewish life and Jewish interests began; and continued right up to the 19th century. In some spheres, both intellectual and economic, Jews were eminent still in the 12th century. It would be difficult to find a sphere in which they were eminent in the 17th. There was a millennium of lost ground to make up, once citizenship could be recovered; and Jews spared no pains to recover it.

As we have already seen in Chapter One, this brought them into the political struggles of the period on the side of the liberal and progressive forces, from whom alone they could hope for their emancipation. But there was no country in which these liberal and progressive forces owed their existence exclusively to Jews, even when individual Jews were prominent among their leaders. The winds of the French Revolution blew in other quarters besides the ghettos of Europe; and the problems of the new industrialism affected others more than Jews.

More profound and far-reaching than the actual struggle for citizenship was the plunge into the new cultural, social and economic life which the removal of medieval restrictions brought in its train. And this involved a sharp conflict within Jewry. It is doubtful whether any rabbi, however orthodox, would have been prepared actually to fight for the restrictions of the ghetto against the obvious human claim to equality. But many viewed with fear and distaste the breakdown of the old ways of life which they foresaw would follow the opening of every avenue to Jewish talents. The Talmud had come to be almost the whole of their intellectual world; and they regarded access to the literature, the science, and the arts of the Gentile as access to forbidden things, a temptation to be steadfastly resisted. But it is not surprising that many of the younger generation refused to follow them, and eagerly absorbed all that they could discover of the strange life around them.

There was, in those days, no "liberal Judaism," to provide them with a spiritual home and background from which they could safely adventure into the new waters. Until a new "conservative" Judaism developed which made some concessions to novelty, the synagogue remained rigidly orthodox; so that those who accepted western European ways of thought were, at first, almost completely cut off from their own community. At the same time, many found it difficult to win wholehearted acceptance in Gentile society. They were forced to become *déracinés*, men without roots, always a class creative of social difficulties. The whole period, however, was so full of change that they were by no means the only men in such a condition. A new bourgeoisie was growing out of the wealth produced by industry, successful men of business, unwillingly accepted into the older society of "gentry," but very conscious of the gulf between themselves and the rest of the class from which they had sprung. But this social tension was not accompanied, as it was in the case of the Jews, by religious or national isolation. Nor were these newly-rich among the British and other western European peoples as distant from the old ways as were inevitably the newly emancipated Jews. They still had some regard for tradition, for ceremony, for the panoply of the dying feudal and ecclesiastical society. So while the Jewish group was, as it were, one hundred per cent, nineteenth century and saw that century as a wholly new world, their fellow radicals among the new middle-class had more limited and practical objectives in their political radicalism, and a more moderate, even half-hearted, hostility to the old order.

It is, therefore, not difficult to understand how those

who hated the new society saw "Jews" everywhere where the new order fought the old; nor, on the other hand, how the emancipated Jews threw themselves sometimes with more enthusiasm than discretion into the battle, just because their boats were burned behind them, and they could not possibly return to, or be incorporated into, the old world of the ghetto and the orthodox synagogue. The world of Jewry was thus even more divided than the rest of western Europe.

The general battle against the supposed influence of the Jews was waged around certain identifiable storm centers. Of these the first, and, throughout the early period the greatest, was the House of Rothschild. The amazing financial success of the five brothers, born in the ghetto of pre-emancipation Frankfurt, and received in all the courts of Europe, was inevitably a subject of legend. Their financial power was, in actual fact, great; their political power was much less than their critics and opponents credited them with. For in the British end of the House inevitably adopted a British attitude, and the Austrian an Austrian attitude, and so on; and these attitudes were often at variance with each other, and cancelled out the political activities of the House. The frantic speculation which inevitably accompanied the uncontrolled expansion of early capitalism, led to many horrid manipulations among the financiers, and many disastrous losses among the speculating public. On both sides of the picture there were, of course, Jews. But only when they were among the first group were they remembered; and their rôle was so exaggerated that *all* financial scandals were assumed to be Jewish, and to be part of a vast web, with the Rothschilds in the center, for the exploitation and impoverishment of Christian Europe. This was the thesis of one of the first books which prepared the way for 19th century antisemitism, *Les Juifs, rois de l'epoque,* by Toussenel.

Another storm center was the press and the world of literature. Jews took readily to journalism, and became prominent to some extent in every country, but particularly in Austria-Hungary. The liberal press was the center of the day-to-day attack on tradition, privilege, and reaction. The attacks were often violent, sometimes unfair. But they were too frequently unanswerable, and thereby only increased the bitterness with which they were resented. It was in this field, perhaps, that Jews, as the most complete and uncompromising representatives of the new trends of the 19th century, earned the bitterest enmity. Was the church attacked? It was not surprising if the most scathing denunciations came from Jewish writers. For what did the church represent to them, but the body which had persecuted their people for centuries? Was it the feudal nobility? Again it represented the power which had locked their ancestors into ghettos. Was it the old learning, and the unreformed universities? They were the bodies which had denied them learning, and those intellectual pursuits always dear to the Jewish people. In a second foundation-work of modern antisemitism, *Le Juif, le Judaisme et la Judaisation des Peuples Chrétiens,* by Gougenot des Mousseaux, this aspect of the question plays a very prominent rôle. Nor would des Mousseaux have found comfort, but the reverse, in the fact that Jewish orthodoxy would be pilloried with the same vigor as non-Jewish tradition by these Jewish journalists and writers.

While the battle was fought with fierceness by the combatants actually engaged, it must not be thought that it occupied the attention of anything but a small minority either of the Jewish or the non-Jewish population. The immense majority, Jewish and other, was occupied with the opportunities of the rapidly expanding economy of the age. A period of expansion is a period of ready tolerance in matters which the business man regards as non-essentials. Political, national and religious questions would all come into such a category. Consequently the majority of western Jews assimilated themselves very successfully into the new environment of their emancipation; developed their businesses, acquired the social outlook of their neighbors, and ignored all wider questions. And the majority of their neighbors, having themselves ample elbow-room for expansion, did the same and regarded Jews with tolerance and indifference. The question of religious distinctions appeared to them an entirely private affair; and the origins of their Jewish neighbors interested them as little as did their own.

Such was the situation up to the year 1881. The appearance of the new political antisemitism a year or two earlier was indeed a danger signal, but its importance was pooh-poohed in sound business circles. The antisemitism of the Russian government was regrettable, but it appeared at first a matter for charitable action and cautious diplomatic intervention. In reality the period of ease and security was over, and European Jewry had entered on the fateful road which led ultimately to the horrors of the Nazi extermination camps of 1942-1944.

Eastern and western Jewish communities differed enormously. In the west were small communities, only in a few capitals exceeding ten thousand souls, whose main ambition, which they were on the way successfully to achieve, was assimilation into the rights and customs of western society. In the east, straggling in a broad belt between the Black and Baltic Seas, under Russian, Austro-Hungarian or Rumanian rule, seven million Jews lived a life in which everything, from

71

details of dress to legal enactments, sharply distinguished them from their neighbors. Only the few hundred thousands in northeastern Austria-Hungary even possessed the beginnings of political equality, and a few score of the wealthy and better educated in Russia, unrestricted freedom of movement in the Russian Empire.

Unlike, ' any of the western Jews these Jews constituted a serious factual problem for the states in which they lived, not by any deliberate choice of their own, but as an ineluctable consequence of the restrictions which fanaticism, fear and hostility imposed, and, since the Russian and Rumanian governments could restrict Jewish occupations but not the Jewish birthrate, the problem augmented instead of diminishing with time. The occupations which these Jews primarily followed were not, as is so often said against them, parasitic, but they were secondary, not always socially valuable, and they offered the means of a decent and stable existence to but a fraction of the Jewish population involved. One very common occupation was certainly a menace both to the Jews and their clients—the retailing of alcohol—but the fault lay, not with the unfortunate inn-keeper, but with the governments and landowners who found it profitable, in more ways than one, to keep their peasants at a level little above that of the animals with whom they shared their miserable cottages.

When an ever-increasing population is rigorously confined by a powerful government to a number of occupations, and to a residential area, totally incapable of providing economic security even of the barest kind for all the inhabitants, the results are bound to be evil. An ever-increasing proportion will live by their wits; and their wits will be driven by the sharp pang of hunger to become both sharper economically, and blunter morally. Moreover poverty and competition will reduce the level of skill and the standard of workmanship even of those reasonably employed. The government, in its turn, confronted by a population whose social value is visibly diminishing will find every excuse in the principles of the loftiest virtue for further increasing the restrictions under which these unhappy subjects live. The radical reforms which alone would have restored their social value, and which could have been based only on political emancipation, a thorough-going educational program, and a complete economic transformation of society, demanded far too vast an effort—both financial and intellectual—for either Rumania or Tsarist Russia. Fine phrases or a new batch of repressive measures took less trouble.

Such was the vicious circle within whose narrowing circumference pullulated the millions of eastern European Jews when, in 1881, they began to pour westward, first in thousands, then in tens, finally in hundreds of thousands from the territories in which they had lived for centuries, but which had become an intolerable prison.

Their coming had two profound effects: they radically transformed the inner life of western European (which includes American) Jewry, and they provided antisemitism with just the new fact of which it stood in need. For these immigrants were essentially foreign; they acquired citizenship politically long before they could be expected to have understood the values and the traditions of the country in which they had come to reside; their presence and their economic standards could easily be represented as a danger to native labor; and their religious and cultural customs shut them off to a large extent from the Christian population. It is not surprising that in the propaganda of antisemitism eastern Jews are well to the forefront.

73

Two causes led to their modifying the whole position of the western Jewries in which they settled. So far as numbers were concerned, it can be said that they swamped them. The assimilated communities of Britain and the United States amounted to about 60,000 and 230,000 respectively in the years before 1880. By 1914 the figures had passed a quarter of a million and a million and three-quarters. Britain and the United States absorbed the largest number of these refugees; but smaller numbers also settled in the dominions and on the continent of Europe. Coming in such numbers, in so short a period—1881-1914—and from so completely different a social and economic environment, it is not surprising that they proved more difficult to assimilate, even in the superficialties of language and external customs. They were much more deeply Jewish in feeling, and they were affected in a completely different way by the growing nationalism of the period. The older members of the western Jewish communities had become citizens before nationalism had become a dominant disease. They, therefore, when they became nationalists, became patriotic Englishmen, Frenchmen, Germans or others. But these new arrivals had become nationalists while they were still living as Jews in an environment which did not desire to assimilate them. Their nationalism, therefore, was Jewish; and this division led to a violent, and still enduring conflict within the Jewish community.

At first the newcomers had no cause but to be grateful for the attitude of the older communities. Even before they had left eastern Europe they had been the object of considerable activity and solicitude on their part. The national and international Jewish organizations, so foolishly and maliciously attacked by anti-semites as 'a secret Jewish world government,' show the Jewish world in one of its noblest and most creditable aspects. No sooner had citizenship been achieved in the west than the newly freed communities turned their thoughts to securing the betterment of conditions among the Jewries of the east. One may laugh at the efforts made by English Jews of the Victorian period to be more English than the English, and similarly in other countries, and their ultra-patriotic assertions that they were absolutely nothing but Englishmen of the Jewish persuasion may have sometimes been ludicrous. But this assertion of patriotism never stood in the way of the recognition of the call of brethren in persecution. Their desire for the emancipation of Russian and Rumanian Jewry, *on the same terms as their own emancipation*—i.e., by a simple grant of individual political rights—was, I believe, a mistaken desire, for the conditions were quite different in the East, and much more than political decisions were needed; but it was wholly sincere, and was the basis of a great deal of costly educational and social work all through eastern Europe, as well as diplomatic and political activity. The *Alliance Israélite Universelle,* and in its train the Board of Deputies of British Jews and the Anglo-Jewish Association, and predecessors of the Hilfsverein Deutschen Juden all rose to meet the tragic situation of the thousands of Jewish refugees who fled from the first pogroms of 1881, not knowing whither they could turn, but possessed of a pathetic faith in the benevolence of the Alliance.

The work of migration was organized and financed entirely from western Jewish sources. A wealthy Austrian Jew, Baron de Hirsch, gave and bequeathed a fund, amounting to several million dollars, with which to acquire land for settlement in South America. The Jewish communities of Britain and America, though they were outnumbered many times by the new arrivals, assumed the full responsibility for their maintenance until they could find productive work; and they financed technical and language classes to help them to establish themselves, and to become competent and independent members of the new societies into which they had been plunged. The work of digesting such large numbers so rapidly was one which would in any case take several generations, and it is not surprising that there was from time to time friction, or that some of the complaints made against the new-comers were justified. It is to the credit of the communities that they neither dissociated themselves from their problem-making brethren, nor relaxed their efforts to turn them into good citizens.

It was as well that the main burden of this work in the 1880's fell on British, French and American Jewries; for those of Germany and Austria were compelled to give a good deal of attention to the business of defending themselves against the now ceaseless attacks of the political antisemites. In this work they were conspicuously less successful. Pamphlet was answered by pamphlet—often by several pamphlets; book was met by books; continual meetings of protest were held; signatures of prominent non-Jews were assiduously collected. But the menace continued to grow, the accusations to become ever more fantastic. The temporary prominence of the House of Rothschild was transformed by the antisemites into a permanent and planned exploitation of the Gentile world; the few successful and prominent Jewish politicians were alleged to be but the façade of a vast Jewish political power—now conservative, and determined to control the wealth and aristocracy of a capitalist society; now revolutionary and determined to undermine the same society. Were the Jews rich, they were called vampires; were they poor, they were accused of undercutting native labor. No accusations were too contradictory, none too extravagant. And the unhappy Jewish leaders, following on behind with their solemn protests, their fervid asseverations, their carefully documented explanations and denials, could never hope to keep pace with the output of accusations which required for their fabrication no more than an exceptionally fertile imagination and an adequate supply of paper.

After 1919 the problems of the Jewish communities of the west became still more complicated. When the new governments of Poland and Rumania signed the minority treaties, it was widely believed that the problem of eastern Jewry was solved. Events soon proved how baseless was this hope. Unfortunately western Jewry still held to its political formula of individual political equality as being the sum total of what was needed, and only small efforts were made—primarily by the great Jewish fund of the U.S.A., the Joint Distribution Committee—to tackle the real economic and social problems which underlay the tensions and hostilities of eastern Europe. The problem was really far vaster than any voluntary fund could possibly solve, and protests—which were continual—only embittered matters still further. From 1933 onward the insidious propaganda and the constant machinations of the Nazis ensured that relations should become still worse, and the economic depressions of those years gave them powerful aid. Then came the flight from Germany itself, and again the communities of the west found themselves called on to raise enormous funds to help the refugees. Few Gentiles realize what efforts were made, and what sums raised, during those years to aid the homeless; and fewer still know that the aid was given to Jew and Christian alike by every Jewish fund, except those dealing with definitely religious purposes. It was not until after the programs of November, 1938, which followed the murder of von Rath in

Paris by an unhappy Jewish student (whose parents had been rendered destitute fugitives in the No-Man's-Land between Germany and Poland) that Jews found themselves so overwhelmed by the calls upon them, that they had to rely on the Christian organizations for the help of Christian refugees.

Although, in fact, the number of these fugitives from Germany was far smaller than those from Russia half a century earlier, the world proved far less able to absorb them. The expanding economy of the 19th century was far more tolerant than the shrinking economy of the inter-war years. In spite of the sacrifices which the Jewish communities made to ensure that the refugees neither interfered with native labor, nor became a charge on the public rates, and in spite of their continual defensive activities against the charges of the antisemites, their situation became more and more precarious. London witnessed antisemitic riots organized by the British Union of Fascists. The whispering campaign against the refugees developed into open attacks in reputable papers; men who detested Nazism made an exception of the Nazi treatment of the Jews; when war came again the whispering of the British Union of Fascists that it was a 'Jewish' war found uncomfortably widespread acceptance among the more ignorant and politically inexperienced section of the community.

The whole work of providing for the refugees had to be conducted under the intolerable searchlight of constant Nazi propaganda, echoed by their jackals in all other countries. There is no people in the world which could have escaped such an ordeal unscathed. None of us are perfect, and our faults differ, so that it is possible for each and all of us to be Pharisees at our neighbors' expense. The uncivilized behavior of many white Americans to negroes, the arrogant attitude of many

Englishmen to 'niggers' and 'dagoes,' the *petites économies* of the French which seem to many other people meanness, all are characteristics at which their neighbors can justifiably point a finger of contempt or hostility. And it is easy to imagine to what a state the world would be reduced if there was an internationally organized, heavily financed body which, in the press, in meetings, in whispering campaigns, set itself steadily to emphasize these characteristics to the exclusion of all else, whenever our relations with each other, and our needs of each other, were delicate or difficult. The same would befall us as has befallen Jewry. Each individual among us—especially those we would least like to be thought representative of our way of life— would be a trustee for all of us. For his failings would be imputed to all of us, and our disclaimer would be rejected. Men would go about saying "some of my best friends are Englishmen" to show their objectivity in relating the latest item of the whispering campaign. And we should be powerless to stop it, for it *is* true that there are Englishmen whose only classification of foreigners is 'niggers' or 'dagoes'; just as there *are* scandals between black and white in America; and the French *do* love their little economies.

In various countries where the law made it possible the Jewish communities have tried to bring their enemies to book before the law—Nazis were frequently condemned in Republican Germany for their slanders on the Jews before 1933—but they have found that a victory in the courts has made no difference to the spread of the libels condemned. The Protocols themselves have been exhaustively examined in several lawsuits, and pronounced forgeries; but their circulation has not sensibly diminished, and their condemnation has not led to any noticeable conversions.

Of course there are Jewish knaves; of course Jewish

leaders have committed mistakes; some of the actions of individuals were unwise; any immigration including some tens of thousands was bound to include some downright criminals; often Jews have protested too violently and too loudly. But there is no rational explanation of how such little and individual affairs could become a menace not only to the Jewish community itself, but to the whole nation in which they constituted scarcely one per cent of the population; no rational explanation of why Jewish defense, which, in the main, was both accurate and reasonable, met with no success comparable to the effort put forth.

Sympathetic and well-intentioned Gentiles frequently asked why 'the Jews did not do something' about some particular scandal. Sometimes there was a real core of fact in the complaint, for any refugee body will cause a certain amount of social friction; more often the scandal was invented and circulated by members of the British Union, or multiplied from a single incident. Few people, who expected the Chief Rabbi or the President of the Board of Deputies to be able at once to suppress anti-social conduct on the part of Jews, would ever have dreamed of expecting the Archbishops of Canterbury or Westminster to accept responsibility for a nominal member of the Anglican or Roman Catholic communions. Jewish leaders and committees worked incessantly for the good name of their community. Every complaint—even the most fatuous—was examined. They had, of course, no legal power; often they could only regret that some things were inevitable so long as men remained imperfect. But all was of little avail. Anti-Jewish feeling had gone beyond the rational stage, even among those who, did they know the actual facts, would have reacted reasonably. But the facts were lost in a cloud of rumor. To understand why the whole world has become "Jew conscious" at the instigation of the Nazi it is necessary to pass from the direct consideration of the Jewish question itself to the study of mass psychology as it affects any minority, and the particular application of that study to the situation of the Jews.

CHAPTER V

THE PSYCHOLOGY AND SOCIOLOGY OF ANTISEMITISM

QUITE recently two organizations in Great Britain, the Society of Jews and Christians, and the Council of Christians and Jews, asked a group of psychologists and sociologists* to prepare them a report on the whole question, and almost simultaneously an American Symposium† on *The Jew in the Gentile World* appeared in which a similar group of American scholars presented a much fuller study of the same subject. There is, then, adequate material to help us to understand why the Jewish question has been so successfully

---

*The actual preparation of the report was entrusted to Dr. Charles S. Myers, late Principal of the National Institute of Industrial Psychology; Dr. Morris Ginsberg, Professor of Sociology, University of London, London School of Economics; Mr. Denys Harding, Lecturer in Psychology, University of Liverpool; Dr. Alec Mace, Professor of Psychology, Birkbeck College, University of London; Major Emmanuel Miller, of the Tavistock Clinic; Major John Rickman, Editor of the British Journal of Medical Psychology; Dr. R. H. Thouless, Head of the Teachers' Training Department, University of Cambridge; Dr. Ranyard West, Department of Psychology, University of Edinburgh. I am grateful to this group for permission freely to make use of their report for the preparation of this section of the book, and a good deal of what follows, especially in the first section, is lifted bodily or summarized, from their work.

†The American study is edited by Dr. Isacque Graeber, formerly of the University of Paris, and Dr. Steuart Henderson Britt, Assistant Professor of Psychology, The George Washington University, in association with sixteen other psychologists and sociologists.

exploited in modern political life and, at the same time, been the subject of so much exaggeration, anxiety and misunderstanding among normally reasonable people.

Fortunately the pattern of group relationships follows in large measure the pattern of individual relationships, so that it is possible for the ordinary man to understand what happens between groups from his own experience as an individual. We are all familiar with the range of emotional feelings which pass through the whole gamut from love to hate, with a neutral point of indifference in their graded path. In some cases we cannot say what it is that provokes these feelings, as for example when individuals fall in love at sight, or in the innate hostile attitude of any dog to any cat. But, fortunately for our present study, in other cases we can find a rational explanation of these emotional feelings. For love and hate are closely associated with another individual or social range of feelings, those which pass from security to insecurity. In many cases the feeling of insecurity is aroused by the presence of something unfamiliar, whether it be something wholly new, or something with which we are already in contact but in which we become aware of new qualities which we do not understand, or which we feel to be outside our control. Towards this novelty we express ourselves in many ways. We may begin by curiosity. If our suspicions are not allayed by the results of our curiosity then we develop a feeling of anxiety and even fear for ourselves, and, simultaneously and proportionate to these feelings, an attitude of suspicion, hatred and anger towards the novelty. It appears as a danger to be circumvented, just as our blood develops functionally anti-bodies to what is new and strange to it. In the case of our blood, once antibodies develop, the blood continues its normal activity, and the danger is removed. The same may happen with regard to an individual or social novelty; or if the two individuals or groups thus brought into contact with each other prove to be approximately equal in size and power, the result may be healthy competition accompanied by respect. If one proves definitely smaller, or, though more numerous, weaker than the other, then associations of mastery and compliance enter, with feelings of domination and submission. When such a situation is accepted by both sides, the social organism becomes again harmonious, as it was in this country when the 'peasant' willingly accepted the superiority of the squire and the 'gentry.'

If any of these things happen it means that the 'minority' has really ceased to be such. It has come to be incorporated in, or accepted by, the society to which it was once strange. But if the novelty continues to retain a separate identity, then the tendency is for the strange individual or group to continue to be regarded hostilely rather than co-operatively. Permanent differences in language, race, religion, culture, dress, diet, etc., can present obstacles, and signify differences in mental attitude, too deep and too unfavorable for friendly, sympathetic communication. Isolation and rivalry or jealousy prove easier than intimate association and co-operation. The basic feeling of insecurity is still present, the fear and anxiety of the majority is bound to be reflected in the minority, and a typical minority situation emerges.

New feelings now come into play, based on the permanence of the minority and its distinctiveness; new mechanisms of the human mind come into operation—feelings which can again be easily recognized in individual experience. The first of these is 'projection'—the mechanism by which things in our own attitude and behavior which we do not like, and do not wish to accept, are projected on to others; as a common example, a quarrel is always the other man's fault. So a minority, which has not been harmoniously accepted, comes early to fulfil the function in the majority group of being blamed for things which the majority has done or suffered, and which offend its moral sense. The moral sense develops early in social evolution. Rudiments of 'conviction of sin' are to be observed even among our domesticated or tamed animals—e.g., the awareness of wrong-doing, the feeling of guilt towards its master of a dog or horse. Among primitive peoples communal guilt or sin is regarded almost as a physical stain which conscience demands shall be removed. Prayers and sacrifices to the gods are not restricted to the desire for fertile crops or successful wars, but are also offered for 'purification' from sin and forgiveness for wrong-doing. Among the early Jews arose the practice of removing the sins of the community by Aaron's transfer of them to the head of a scapegoat which was then led away into the wilderness to be released there in an appropriate domain of evil spirits. The goat bore the stains formerly carried by the human community; the fault or blame was laid on it.

In the course of the development of society throughout the world sin came also to be transferred by being projected on to a minority human group; on whom, in a rather different sense and manner, the blame was laid for the sins or for the misfortunes, failures or defects of the larger community, and for the famine, pestilence, political unrest, etc., with which the majority were supposed to be divinely visited. In early days the Christians suffered from this same 'projection' in the Roman Empire. In a famous passage, the Church Father, Tertullian, cries: "If the Tiber overflows into the city, if the Nile does not flow into the countryside, if the heavens remain unmoved, if the earth quakes, if there is famine or pestilence, at once the cry goes up:

'To the lions with the Christians'." The minority group was held responsible. It was accordingly cruelly, even murderously, attacked; and it came to be regarded as the majority's bitterest enemy. Hatred became an excuse for further suspicions, just as guilt became an excuse for further fears. Thus a minority group became hated not only because it was thought to display evil characteristics; evil characteristics were further sought in it because it was hated.

In addition to projection, there is a second mechanism known as 'displacement' which affects alike individual and group relationships. In displacement we direct a pent-up emotion to an objcet other than its original target. We 'take it out on the dog,' usually because we fear the consequences of taking it out on its original cause—the government whose regulations irk us, the employer who refuses our requests, the wife who burns the kippers. In the same way we blame a minority when things go wrong with us, if we cannot, or fear to, put them right ourselves. When these two mechanisms, projection and displacement, have come into play to embitter relations between two individuals or groups, there steps in a third to quiet our consciences on the subject—'rationalization.' We invent a justifiable and respectable reason for our true motives and feelings, and, equally, a disreputable and discreditable reason for the activities of the minority. If a man beats us at business by being cleverer or harder working than we are, we do not like to admit this, and so find a discreditable reason for his success, and consequently, a justification for blaming him for it.

All these feelings are equally applicable to individual or to group relationships, because, in fact, once we are considering a minority in this light, it is treated as an individual in the sense that differences within the minority are not recognized. All are treated as alike.

If this is too glaringly absurd, then it will be insisted that any member of the minority who shows different characteristics is an exception. We all know the kind of remarks which begin with "some of my best friends are Jews but. . . ." But the picture which is drawn will not merely deal with the minority as though it were a single individual. It will also inevitably be a simplification, and so to some extent a caricature, of the supposed characteristics of the minority. It could not be otherwise, for a 'type' cannot have too subtle and complicated characteristics, or it would cease to be useful as a type. We are in fact only doing with the minority the same thing as we constantly do with other things. If we mention a lawyer, a parson, a chorus girl, or even a house or a chair, it conveys a definite idea of what we mean, based on a few clear-cut characteristics, even though they are almost certainly inaccurate about the particular specimen of the type we are referring to.

In actual fact in all human groups the variations within the group are bigger than its divergencies from other groups. We say that "Norwegians are tall," but statistically the variations in height among Norwegians are greater than the difference between the average height of a Norwegian and that of any other normal human group. The same is true of the mental and moral characteristics of any minority. In fact they vary enormously. But once they become the subject of our 'projection,' or 'displacement,' or 'rationalization,' all members of the minority are assumed to have similar recognizable characteristics.

When the minority is actually not too dissimilar from ourselves, and especially if it is not living a separate life segregated from the rest of the population, this already simplified picture will receive a further and serious distortion. The virtues of the minority and its estimable members will be identified with the majority. It is a natural human characteristic to identify ourselves with that which we admire. If we admire courage, and we are English, we like to hear stories of courageous Englishmen, and if we hear of a gallant incident, we are sure the hero of it is English. If we know he isn't we say: "he might almost be an Englishman." If we are good local patriots, we take pride in the famous men from our town or village. We feel they belong to us, and we share in their reflected glory. It is extraordinary to what lengths people will sometimes go to find a link between themselves and something or someone they admire. Relics with 'historical association' are eagerly sought after—the bed in which Queen Elizabeth slept, the table at which Queen Victoria had tea—and the man whose brother had once been gardener in a house at which Field-Marshal Montgomery's aunt had stayed for a night would probably find the relationship good enough to justify him in relating the entire incident at length to any audience rash enough to give him an opening.

In the same way when a member of a minority performs some action or exhibits some characteristic we admire, we think not of his membership of the minority, but of something else in him whereby we can link him to ourselves. His son was at the same school as our nephew; he was born in the same town as we were; and in any case he is at once "English." The war has provided innumerable experiences of this phenomenon in the case of the Jews. The press has constantly published details of black-marketers when the names were foreign or Jewish, because the ordinary reader could then feel that none of the shame of the offense fell on him. But if a Jew performs a meritorious action, or wins a decoration, it is the rarest thing for the press to draw attention to his Jewishness. And if his name happens to be English—as in the case of Major

Wigram, inventor of battle drill and killed with guer-
illas in Italy, or Harry Errington, winner of the George
Cross—he is never associated with the Jews at all.
He is another English hero and we are all proud of
him. In other words, when the minority cannot be automatically distinguished by the fact that it leads a completely segregated life, or is totally dissimilar physically
from the majority, the picture drawn of its character
and activities will be based almost wholly on those
traits in the minority from which the majority wishes to
dissociate itself, and will completely ignore all qualities
of the opposite character.

What has been described so far is the normal psychological situation which any group has to face which
wishes to retain its identity as a minority within a
larger society. This does not, of course, mean that all
the various psychological mechanisms described will
continually be brought into play against it. It will not
be constantly punished by the 'projections' of the
majority, traduced by their 'transferences' or ravaged
by their 'rationalizations.' This is equally true of group
and of individual relations. But in both cases when a
situation arises which calls these psychological mechanisms into play, it will be on an identifiable 'stranger'
or minority that they will be most likely to be dis-
charged.

What has been so far described is also independent
of the actual character and activities of the minority
itself. The various individual reactions to a 'stranger'
were based simply on his strangeness, and would have
been unaffected by his virtues or vices. But this cannot
be the whole story in anything as complex as the
relations of two historical human groups. They do
have actual group characteristics, and, quite factually,
these group characteristics may provoke pleasure or
displeasure on the part of others with whom they come

into contact. An obvious example of this was the trouble between the country folk and the 'Londoners' in the period of mass evacuation. Much rumor, exaggeration and invention was built up on an actual substratum of real differences. And the same will be found to be true when we come to deal with the Jews as a minority.

There is yet one final factor to be considered. Where a majority-minority relationship is permanent, neither the majority nor the minority remain exactly as they were before. Both are affected by the strains and consequences of this specially charged relationship. The traditional attitude of the retired Anglo-Indian to 'niggers' and servants is an example of the increase of arrogance on the part of the dominant group (in this case equivalent to the 'majority'), and the equally traditional attitude of the Chinese to the 'foreign devil' is an example of the increase of suspicion on the part of the majority. In both cases anxiety and insecurity play a considerable part in evoking these characteristics.

The minority is, of course, similarly, but probably more deeply, affected. So far as the majority is concerned, its attitude to a minority will be only one of the matters engaging its interests, and determining its character. But the behavior to it of the majority has such a profound and all-embracing effect on the life of the minority, that it will be much more strongly affected by the nature of the minority-majority relationship. How completely a minority may change its previous character under this new influence is shown for example, in the physical and mental deterioration of the Indians on the American and Canadian Reserves. So extreme a deterioration is, however, only likely to occur when the minority has abandoned every hope of ever recovering its former freedom or status, and has no inner resources wherewith to meet its new position.

The Negro slave must have felt as hopeless as the American Indian, but he saved himself from the latter's deterioration long before the hope of emancipation appeared over the horizon, by the development of new qualities—gentleness, religious escapism, personal loyalty to his master—which he can scarcely have shown in his native Africa.

A minority which has not abandoned hope will make every effort to keep alive and to strengthen those elements on which its hope is based. It will develop pride in its own traditions; and this will often be offset by contempt for the culture of the majority which possesses the physical power over it; it will concentrate on the field in which it feels itself superior, and develop a philosophy to support that superiority. At the same time, while this is fermenting in its inner life, it will conceal it from members of the majority, towards whom it will develop an attitude of compliance and submissiveness. It will therefore scarcely escape the charge of insincerity and obliquity in its dealings; and the majority will still feel the fear based on insecurity in its dealings with it, for it will feel that there is something there which it does not understand. So, in a typically vicious circle, the feelings on either side will be deepened and intensified. It is an example of what can be generally recognized in any sphere—school, home or factory—that excessive power on one side and excessive dependence on the other cause various kinds of deterioration to both parties.

The Jews as a Minority

In the case of the Jews it will easily be seen how completely they fill the rôle of a 'minority,' and how they have this characteristic, peculiar to themselves, that they are everywhere a minority. Everywhere therefore they are subjected to the same possibilities of psychological reaction on the part of majorities; and in consequence the typical picture of a Jewish minority drawn by the majority in one country is 'confirmed' by the discovery that the picture in another country is exactly the same. Of course there are common features in the Jewish character and tradition everywhere, but this confirmation of a caricature which inherently is based, not on Jewish characteristics, but on the way in which a majority draws a minority, makes it peculiarly difficult for the public in any country to see what really is the nature of its Jewish minority, and what actual problems, if any, are involved in its presence.

On the basis of the general examination of minorities as such, it is also possible to see why antisemitism has so suddenly spread, and why Hitler's technique was so successful. Hitler created a world-wide feeling of insecurity, and all the feelings associated with insecurity came into play. In such times the sense of danger causes a group to coalesce and close its ranks; and its fears make it look with suspicion on the outsider. In the times of prosperity and stability before 1914 the civilized world had shown a wide measure of toleration and capacity to absorb new elements. It had relatively easily digested the several million Jews who fled from Tsarist Russia between 1881 and 1914. Between 1933 and 1939 the situation had so changed that it could not digest the few hundred thousand Jews and others who sought refuge from Nazi persecution; and old, established minorities, not merely Jews, who had previously felt perfectly secure, suddenly found themselves isolated and mistrusted.

This, however, is not the whole story. Although the political antisemitic movement only dates from 1879, and its modern form from 1933, the problem of Jewish relations with the majorities among which they lived goes much further back than that; and the success with which modern antisemites have done their work would have been impossible without that long inheritance behind them.

When in times of prosperity conflicts such as those between a majority and a minority tend to disappear from the surface, they are not thereby dissolved or eliminated from the body politic, any more than the complex of an individual is rendered harmless by disappearing underground into his subconscious. So old pictures of Jewish behavior, some religious, some social, some economic, still lingered in the memories of the peoples. Nor was it these pictures alone which aided the task of the antisemites. It has already been said that the dominance-submission relationship in individuals or groups alters their previous character on each side, usually for the worse. So past *attitudes* remained as much as past pictures, waiting to be resurrected at a touch.

These pictures and attitudes as between Jew and non-Jew are not only world-wide in extent, since the Jews are dispersed throughout the world, they are also profoundly ingrained into the mentalities of Jew and non-Jew since they may have arisen at any point in the almost forty generations of the dispersed life of Jewry as a group of scattered minorities. It is therefore quite Utopian to expect that they can be effectively dealt with in a few years simply by legislation, or by uninformed good-will. That, however, is no excuse for inaction. It is rather a demand that we begin now, for we have a long road to travel, and, until we reach a good deal nearer our destination, we cannot insure that future anti-democratic, anti-progressive movements will not be able to exploit anti-Jewish feeling as successfully as their predecessors in our own and previous generations.

The Sociological and Psychological Problem of Jewry

ALL of us, whatever the strength of our individualities, are largely conditioned by two factors external to ourselves—our heredity and our environment. It is, of course, the same with the Jews. Jews are the product of a heredity of which the central factor is Judaism, and of an environment of which the central factor has been, for nearly two thousand years, dependence on others for their political situation and even their right of residence. The first question, then, which we shall need to answer is: Have both of these influences contributed to our problem? Do both need modification before any solution can be achieved?

The importance of this question lies in the fact that there is tremendous ignorance of the nature of Judaism in the general community, and that antisemitic agencies constantly spread the idea that it is Judaism itself which makes the Jews an intolerable burden to any community which receives them.

A religious inheritance is conditioned by the history through which it passes, so that we can expect traces in Judaism of the effects of the psychological mechanisms already discussed. They will be found especially in two fields. There is first the concept of the "Chosen People," and closely linked with that is an attitude of contempt for the Gentile. Secondly there is the rationalization of the actual doing of harm to the Gentile 'enemy.'

To some extent the concept of being a "chosen people" is shared by everyone. I know no nation which delights to proclaim its inferiority to others! Moreover pride in an ancient tradition is an essential balance to the feeling of inferiority which oppression inevitably breeds in a minority. This also we find in many other peoples—the Czechs and Poles for example. So far as

the Jews are concerned it is more than doubtful if the
'chosen people' concept, while it may irritate a few,
could be shown to be much of a problem in modern
times. On the one hand it has been diverted within
Jewry itself to the healthy enthusiasm of rebuilding a
Jewish civilization in the National Home; and on the
other, in so far as it retains its religious and non-
aggressive meaning, it is merged into the larger
struggle of theistic religion for recognition within a
world which is increasingly sceptical of religious values. To Christians at any rate there must always be a
profound element of truth in the belief in a religious
mission within Jewry; and a church which surrenders
its own consciousness of a Jewish inheritance is on its
way to a complete surrender to Nazism.

The reaction of contempt for the non-Jew is probably a somewhat more serious element in difficulties
between the Jewish and non-Jewish population. It also
has an origin in the historical development of Judaism.
All religions in their primitive stages exhibit this contempt—some branches of Christianity, such as the
Roman Catholics in Spain, are still at this stage of
development. It is to be found in the Old Testament;
and it is to be found in rabbinic literature. It flourished
in periods when Jewry felt its pagan environment men-
acing it on all sides. In the modern world its roots lay in
the orthodox Jewry of eastern Europe which, through
migration, has provided so large a proportion of the
members of western Jewish communities. In eastern
Europe it was kept alive by the contempt which a
people with a respect for learning had for the ignorance of administrators who oppressed them and the
superstition of mobs who attacked them. An orthodox
Jew in those conditions might teach his children to spit
at passing a church; even in this country he may refuse
to allow the name of Christ to be mentioned in the

pulpit of his synagogue. He still lives virtually a ghetto life, the strictness of his dietary laws forbidding anything but the most superficial intercourse with the Gentile community. This type is growing much rarer in the Jewish world, but there is apt to remain in the non-Orthodox Jew something of this aversion or, at least, contempt. Actually one would expect it to be much stronger than it is, when one thinks of the hatred of the Poles for the Russians based on the humiliations and persecutions of Tsarist days, or of many of the other hatreds, religious and political, in Europe. That it is not so in the Jewish case is due to two reasons. Even from a purely psychological standpoint, the aversion or contempt which the Jewish minority might feel is balanced by the optimism and ambition which are characteristic of the Jewish mentality. Desire to emulate and be accepted by the majority cancels out in many cases the alternative minority feelings. To this must be added that the religious tradition of Judaism, while it does contain some element of the exclusiveness and intolerance common to most religions, contains also an emphasis on tolerance and universalism which, in view of its antiquity, is almost peculiar to itself. From the beginning Jews were taught in their Scriptures to regard the stranger—the minority group, from their point of view—in just the same way as they regarded members of their own group. "The stranger that dwelleth with you shall be unto you as one born among you and thou shalt love him as thyself; for ye were strangers in the land of Egypt" (Lev. xix, 34). Further, they were taught that their God was the God of all the earth and that all men were his children. "Have we not all one father? Hath not one God created us? (Malachi, ii, 10).

This element has also had a salutary effect on the second, and more serious, characteristic of Judaism considered as a minority religion—religious justification of doing evil to the outside enemy or oppressor. There is nothing surprising in the desire of slaves of Pharaoh to "spoil the Egyptians," or in the extreme vengeances which early Hebrew prophets pronounced in the name of their religion on Philistines, Amalekites and others. Similar incidents can be gleaned from the history of all religions which have willingly discovered religious sanctions for the angers, fears and hatreds of their members. The attitude of Protestants and Catholics to each other in 16th and 17 century European history provides a much more recent example of this than the usually quoted stories of the ancient Hebrews!

In so far as the Jews are concerned, it is not so much the Bible that provides the basis for the belief that Jews are bound to work for the destruction of Gentiles, as the quotations which have been produced in anti-semitic publications from much less accessible and little known "rabbinical" texts, such as the Talmud. They win easy acceptance among non-Jews, for the ordinary man, when not moved by some higher ideal, lives his own life on the basis of doing good to his friends, and doing harm to his enemies, and takes this as being completely 'natural' and proper. He therefore finds no difficulty in believing that Jews do the same, with this difference—that he knows that Christianity disapproves of such conduct, so that what shocks him is not that Jews should behave as he does himself, but that the Jews' religion should (as he thinks) support them in doing so.

It is a great pity that most people are so ignorant of the development of Judaism, for its treatment of this particular problem provides a fascinating study for sociologists and all who are concerned with the bettering of human relations. It brings out clearly the peculiar feature of Judaism, that it is a religion whose leaders have been scholars and intellectuals—men of the types we would associate with teachers and lawyers—not ecclesiastical 'imperialists' of the type of the great Popes and Archbishops, or fervent preachers, like the great 'revivalists.' The problem itself is, of course, common to all societies. We all tend to like our friends and hate our enemies, and unless we can develop the former and deter the latter feeling we cannot get much social progress. Judaism, having a very ancient literature, had, as already said, plenty of examples of the latter feeling being vigorously expressed, with few inhibitions, in its earlier documents. The first method the rabbis adopted to cope with it is one with which, without knowing it, we are familiar from the Sermon on the Mount. When Jesus Christ told the people "Ye have heard what was said of old time . . . but I say unto you" it is often suggested that He is here making a contrast between His new teaching and Judaism. This is not so. He is using the method the rabbis had evolved for the same purpose. They taught: 'Ye have heard what was said of old time . . .'—then they quoted the spoiling of the Egyptians, the massacre of the Amalekites and so on—'but learn also to say . . .' and then followed some other passage from the Bible which in fact contradicted it—for example Proverbs xxv, 21 and 22, "If thine enemy be hungry, give him bread to eat; and if he be thirsty, give him water to drink: For thou shalt heap coals of fire upon his head, and the Lord shall reward thee."

But they did not attack the problem only at this level. As one would expect from the type of leadership in Judaism they dealt with it also by an appeal at all levels. At the highest they emphasized the universality of God's rule and His concern for the 'stranger' as much as for the Jew: at an easier level for ordinary men, they reminded them of the extreme imprudence of such behavior towards those who had it in their power to do more than reply. They advised good treatment of the stranger and outsider "for the sake of peace"; and they then united the two appeals by reminding men that peace was an essential characteristic of God, and not merely a matter of self-interest.

Moreover the rabbis wisely played on one instinct in order to control another; they played on the optimism which has been one of the most striking Jewish characteristics, by reminding their hearers that they were more likely to win the approval of their neighbors by more prudent conduct, and that without this approval, their position was extremely insecure. This also they linked, at a higher level, with the need to win the approval of the Gentiles for the Jewish belief in God. We are less accustomed to this combination of approaches within a single religious teaching, and forget that the Founder of Christianity, in a truly Jewish spirit, advised His followers to be wise as serpents, as well as harmless as doves.

In the result the rabbis were extraordinarily successful, and it is noticeable that those antisemites who seek for quotations to prove the contrary either have to go to extremely remote times, or to find quotations from periods, of almost intolerable strain, which they then carefully separate from their context.

That no Jew has ever done what harm he could to a non-Jew it would be absurd to maintain; but that he has done so in despite of his religious teaching and tradition is unquestionable.

In the wilder antisemitic propaganda there are also much more serious accusations against Judaism, even to the extent of asserting that it demands the ritual murder of Gentiles and the use of their blood; and that there is a world-wide Jewish plot for the destruction of Christianity and the domination of all Gentile peoples. To this kind of statement it is only possible to make a complete denial. They have not been supported by evidence which stands a moment's examination by any competent non-Jewish scholar.

We are in much surer ground, and much nearer the heart of things, when we look to Jewish history rather than Judaism to find the explanation of the difficuties created by Jews as minorities. But we must look at the matter from the standpoint of the sociologist as much as from that of the psychologist. For the mere fact of living together and of living in a certain atmosphere—physical or mental—has as much effect as the particular results of the majority-minority nexus.

This is particularly true of the contemporary Jewish problem. One of the commonest accusations against the Jews, and one which rests on sufficient factual evidence to make a good foundation for further anti-semitic exaggeration and distortion, is the charge of practicing a lower business morality. It is not primarily a charge of *breaking* the law (I am not talking now of war-time accusations of black-marketing, etc.) but of sharp practice just within the law, of finding ingenious loopholes and methods of sailing close to the wind. To understand this situation we have to go back to the fact that the majority of Jewish business men in western Europe or America are at most two generations removed from life in Tsarist Russia, and we need to understand the totally different reactions to the idea of law which conditions in Tsarist Russia and in democratic countries would produce in anybody. By and large, our commercial law is produced by our commercial community, through the members of Parliament who largely represent its interest, and it is administered by judges who enjoy the confidence of the community. Our normal tradition is, therefore, that the law is something in whose making we have had a hand, and which we accept and observe, and expect the other man to observe. And such is the situation in other democratic countries. But such was not the situation in Tsarist Russia. The laws came entirely from above and from outside. They carried with them no moral compulsion, they obtained no instinctive acceptance. Moreover, so far as the Jews were concerned, they were often deliberately designed, not to aid, but to hamper the earning of an honest livelihood. They were restrictive and oppressive.

One or two examples of the position created after 1881, when the Jews began to flee westward, will make the situation clear. Those given are not taken from a Jewish source but from the work of a great French Liberal, Anatole Leroy-Beaulieu.* A Jewish girl, who wished to go to Moscow to learn shorthand, could only avoid expulsion from the city as a Jewess by registering as a public prostitute. She was then at the mercy of the police if she did not follow her registered 'profession' for the police's benefit. If a Jew went to the country for a holiday or convalescence, that constituted an "official change of residence," and he could not then assume any right to return to the place in which he had previously lived. As a Jew might not live in a village, the administration would suddenly declare a town in which a number of Jews resided to be administratively a village. The Jews then had to leave —or bribe the police. And so on and so on. Legislation of a similar character dealt with their economic activities, their official identity papers, their duty to perform military service, even their religious customs. Is it surprising that their conceptions of a law and a policeman were very different from that of the home-born Englishmen among whom they settled?

*Les Juifs de Russie, Recueil, Paris, 1891.

The penalties involved in law-breaking would create a tendency to keep the letter, though even here the venality of administrators encouraged bribery. But, the letter kept, there was no moral inhibition against discovering methods of evasion. It was a battle of wits between the Jewish business man and the police and administration—and this would be a very unfair description of the normal attitude of tens of thousands of business men in this country, whatever their peccadilloes, and their occasional vast frauds. Further, successful fraud earns no admiration in a country such as ours, except among men who are themselves dishonest. In Tsarist Russia, however, the man who managed to outmaneuver a hundred petty restrictions and hostile officials and carry on a thriving business earned the admiration of his neighbors. In other words the decent Jewish business man, not the minority who were deliberately crooked, came to this country and to similar western countries, with a mind attuned to an entirely anti-social conception of law, and sharpened by generations of experience, to look at a law not from the standpoint of how honorably to observe it, but how ingeniously to evade it. It takes some generations to eradicate such a tradition, and in the meantime, Jewish businesses as such will tend to be suspect by their Gentile competitors; and the numbers of cases in which individual Jewish business men are rightly suspected by their Gentile competitors of sharp practice which just does not break the law, will be somewhat higher than normal. It is a problem which time will solve, and is, in fact, solving. Accusations of a similar type have, in similar circumstances, been once justified against other groups, whom now nobody would think of accusing of an innate tendency to dishonorable practices. The situation in the U.S.A. after Prohibition should remind us how easily illegality may come to be socially approved.

Closely linked to this problem is another, which is more directly related to their situation in the country of their arrival than to that in the country of their departure. The Jews, as a minority and as newcomers, are rarely able to find places for themselves in the old, established and most highly respected professions and occupations. They are left to seek an entry either into those occupations which are less highly esteemed and less securely established, or into those in which novelty and energy are the main pre-conditions to success. In such occupations labor conditions are often less carefully, or not at all, regulated, business codes and conventions less well established and accepted, and opportunities for exploitation and speculation more frequent. It is easy to remember only this side and to forget that such occupations demand a high degree of initiative, energy and imagination, and that in the end the whole community may profit from these qualities. When these occupations are in the hands of a minority, then, by the mechanisms already described, it is particularly likely that only the bad side—the "sweat-shops" of the East End, the swindles in hire purchase, and so on—will be remembered, and remembered long after they have possibly ceased to have any general factual existence.

Side by side with such occupations we need to consider the position of the less numerous, but more influential, professions. Two particularly affect the Jews, medicine and law, for these have been followed by Jews for centuries. Their particular attraction in the 19th century, however, was the fact that they were *free* professions, in which a man could make his way by his own energies and abilities. So many of the other middle-class occupations were closed, either by law or custom (e.g., the army and civil service in many countries) that the number of sons of Jewish immigrants who turned to these two was enough to make them a noticeable group both in the universities and in afterlife. But even here the way forward was not as easy as for the son of a native-born of comparable talent, and the newcomer found himself looking for marginal activities, the novelties and the experiments, in order to establish himself; and when he could not find such, he was driven to trying to get clients away from other practitioners, by methods which the latter, naturally enough, quickly and sometimes rightly condemned as "unethical practice."

In considering the situation of any minority, and this is painfully true of the situation of the Jews, activities which alienate not merely the business rival or the unreflecting, but the more sensitive members of the majority, cause by far the most damage. They silence the defense, and estrange the support of those most likely to raise their voices against prejudice or persecution. The various professions concerned with the entertainment of the public are a conspicuous example of this. It is a field in which a capacity to invent novelty is far more important than a well established tradition. It is therefore a field into which newcomers are likely to gravitate, for they have just as much chance of success as anybody else. Unhappily it is also a field in which, especially in a disintegrating society such as contemporary western civilization, the demand for novelty is likely to be a demand also for ever cruder and less healthy and creative forms of recreation. A vast public, with increased money and leisure, but with less roots in either religion or culture, demands simply to be amused by an appeal to its most primitive, unsocial and animal instincts. Boxing becomes less of a science and more of an exhibition of blood and brutality; the drama, represented almost wholly by the movies, relies only on sex and escapist adventure, on crime and thrills; gambling, in all forms, prospers. In the higher income levels equally vicious amusements find plenty of patrons. Select gambling clubs, flashy hotels and bars, night clubs and so on, attract a numerous public, perhaps more 'educated' but equally empty in so far as any purpose pervades their lives or any moral standard dictates their conduct. Now it is ridiculous to accuse the purveyors of amusement of responsibility for the fact that society is in this condition and desires and supports these forms of entertainment. But those who provide them can naturally look for no defense from those who are struggling for the expression of a wholly different conception of society, based on wholly different standards, religious or humanistic.

Statistically the Jews involved in these various amusements are not merely a minority within these occupations, but they are also an infinitely small proportion of the Jewish people. But statistics play little part in the creation of human emotions. It is enough for the numbers just to be sufficient to draw the attention of a public, already sensitive and suspicious, for them to play their part in accentuating a minority problem. But the antisemitic explanation of these activities of Jews, that it is part of a deliberate plot to debauch the Gentile world, would only need to be considered, if there were not a much simpler and more natural explanation of why Jews are to be found in these activities, one moreover which we can see to be valid in a field which has nothing whatever to do with the Jews.

The explanation is the morally disintegrating effect of having no roots and no standards. Moscow knew it with tens of thousands of orphan children after the last war; parts of London know it now, and similar situations are to be found wherever human beings are uprooted from their past environment and received into no effective substitute. There may be some among us so strong that we can maintain a high moral standard without any external or economic assistance. But most of us would admit that membership of a Church, of a local community in which we were known, of a family or of a profession, kept us straight when, in our weaker moments, we were tempted to some act which our normal standards of behavior condemned; and that if it were not for these social checks, we could not be sure that we would have resisted the temptation. It is a variant of the stock remark of the detective in the thriller: "Most of us would commit at least one murder if we were sure we couldn't be found out," only it is fear of the disapproval and condemnation of those among whom we live, rather than fear of the rope, which is operative with us. The tremendous migrations of the Jewish people in the last half century, the entirely strange environment in which they found themselves, and the hostility which they encountered very often on their arrival in a new country—these are enough to explain why a number of people without roots and without standards may be found among some sections of the Jewish people.

A further problem which is sociological in origin, and which is apt to affect all minorities, is that their numbers are distorted by the unequal way in which they are distributed throughout the new community. If, for example, they are all agricultural pioneers in a new country with plenty of land, this concentration of their numbers into a single occupation creates no problem; it draws attention to them in a way which earns rather the commendation of the majority. But the Jews have never been in this position. They never entered a country as landless peasants, but either as merchants or as industrial proletarians. But even within the cities they tended to concentrate into a few occupations and districts in which they quickly became prominent. Both are natural. All immigrants tend to carry the occupation of their previous existence into their new environment, and Jews came from a very restricted range of occupations; further all large groups of immigrants tend to settle near to each other for social life, fellowship and a sense of protection.

A great deal of the fear of 'Jewish domination' is linked to this inequality of distribution. For the majority sees where the minority is present, but forgets where it is absent. Much of the Fascist propaganda in every country makes use of this fear; and, by confusing 'prominence' with 'domination,' by carefully selecting its evidence, and by tacitly assuming that if there are a number of Jews in a profession they not only 'dominate' it, but dominate it to the national disadvantage, they have caused serious alarm to ordinary decent citizens, who are made to feel that their national way of life is actually endangered by the presence of these 'foreign' bodies.

From these sociological aspects of the question we can return to some more directly psychological factors affecting the situation, factors all arising in different ways from the basic feeling of insecurity and its consequences. If we study the story of the Jews in the Old Testament, and in the Roman Empire, we cannot help being struck by the differences between the characteristics there displayed, and those made familiar to us in more recent history. In Palestine the Jews were a people of aggressive and warlike character; they fought violently for their religion and for their liberty; on two occasions they challenged the whole might of the Roman Empire, and it took the most seasoned soldiers and the most expert generals' campaigns lasting several years to crush them. They were "stiff-necked" and "rebellious." In modern times they are represented rather as sycophantic, cringing, submissive. The change is due to the dispersion; to the new relationships created by becoming minorities subject to the will of the majorities among whom they lived. In the same way the son of an aggressive father learns by stern parental discipline to suppress and to repress an inherited (or imitated) aggressiveness and is forced obsessionally into an outward accommodating gentleness towards others, beyond what is natural for him, so that he earns a reputation for sycophancy and obliquity in his dealings. But the original aggressiveness will be likely to come out in some way or other. In the case of an individual it may appear in periodic outbursts of bullying; in the case of a minority it must usually seek other forms. With the Jews it comes out in the aggressive social behavior which is so frequent a complaint against those who have newly come to countries in which they are legally and socially free, from countries, such as Hitlerite Germany or Tsarist Russia, in which they were socially and legally oppressed.

Where the background of oppression is particularly strong and insidious, a minority is likely to suffer—as is an individual—from a 'persecution mania,' a constant conviction that they are being persecuted, and that the most innocent action has a sinister hostile meaning. This feeling has been particularly embarrassing in dealing with refugees from Nazism, because it was linked to an actual Nazi world organization of espionage and intimidation—the *Antisemitische Weltdienst* of Erfurt—which gave a substantial background of painful reality to the most imaginary fears. But these fears, even when imaginary, made acceptance by the majority doubly difficult and sometimes impossible. The victim saw unfriendliness everywhere; the most genuine offers of friendship and assistance were repelled; or, on the other hand, accepted with such demands upon the time and spiritual energy of those who tried to assist that it was more than they could cope with. All the refugee organizations, as well as many private homes which have offered hospitality, have had pitiful experience of this effect of fear and insecurity.

When a minority is in this situation, it exhibits another characteristic, which makes a vicious circle of its isolation. It dare not accept the most friendly and sympathetic criticism, lest acceptance should be used as grounds for further oppression, or further misrepresentation. It gets itself into the ridiculous position of appearing to the majority to be claiming an almost superhuman virtue, and thereby still further alienates its sympathy.

Such are the considerations, sociological and psychological, which constitute the real Problem with which we have to deal. The stock in trade of the professional antisemite—Jewish 'control' of governments, finance, business, professions, this, that and the other—do not need consideration from the factual point of view. As facts they are myth. The evidence for their truth would not be accepted by any reasonable man for a moment, were it not for the obsessions, distortions and exaggerations which are implied in the relationship between a majority and a minority, especially when a good deal of the latter is of relatively recent foreign origin.

Having thus looked at the situation as a sociologist and a psychologist might look at it when they are considering the Jews as a minority, it will be worth looking now at the contemporary Jewish community itself, as either of these two scientists might consider it if he were considering it by itself, and not in its relations with the majority. For the picture which has been produced so far is, of course, partial, often to the extent of being a caricature.

CHAPTER VI

JEWISH COMMUNITIES OF THE WORLD TODAY

IT will not be possible to say how many Jews there are in the world until we know more accurately the figures of the Nazi massacres throughout Europe, from western France to eastern Poland and the Ukraine. In 1939 there were altogether about 16 million. Since 1939 it is known that more than four million have perished unnaturally, by starvation, disease, and murder in every terrible form. The community on which the heaviest blow has fallen is that of Poland. In 1939 it amounted to about 3,400,000; to-day, even including a million who have found refuge in Soviet territory, it is certain that less than half remain alive. In the post-war world the significant Jewish communities will be those of the U.S.A. (about 4,750,000) the U.S.S.R. (3,000,000, including those who have entered since 1939), the National Home in Palestine (550,000), and possibly that of Great Britain (430,000, including refugees from Nazi Germany). Almost everywhere the Jewish birth rate is lower than that of the general population of the country where they live, so that, by and large, the surviving Jewish population is likely to remain constant for some time to come.

In one of his brilliant short stories (*The Village that Voted the Earth was Flat*) Kipling describes how three men revenged themselves on the village of Huckley by making it world-famous, although there was no real foundation for any of the stories they invented about it. When their work was completed they returned to look at Huckley, and were surprised and disappointed to find it was just the ordinary and uninteresting village it was before they started to work on it. The same experience would come to anyone who, after hearing of the Jews from the speeches and literature of the anti-semites, or knowing something of their history over the millennia, actually comes into close contact with a Jewish community. They are such ordinary people; and where he observes differences they arise from such ordinary causes—causes he knows to be operative among all other ordinary people—their history, their environment, their hopes and ambitions, the way they are treated, their individual loves and hates and fears, their religion, their politics, their citizenship.

The common feature of all Jewries is urbanization. Centuries of exclusion from the land had made the Jews town-dwellers before other Europeans. The 19th century intensified everywhere the drift to the towns among the whole population, and the 20th century witnessed the growth of mammoth capital cities. Both these movements are reflected in Jewry, to the extent that about a quarter of all the Jews of the world lived in 1933 in the nine capital cities of New York, Budapest, Buenos Aires, Kiev, London, Moscow, Paris, Vienna and Warsaw. Each of these communities was over 100,000, and that of New York around 2,000,000. In many of these cities Jews, especially the more recent arrivals, were usually concentrated into certain districts. It is undoubtedly these two facts which have lent color to the exaggerated pictures often given of the number of Jews in any one country.

As an urban population they show the normal urban preference for the white collar professions. It is only

112

in a few Jewries that a different tendency is manifest. In the U.S.S.R. there has been a definite move into heavy industry among the younger Jews; and in the National Home Jews are to be found in every occupation including agriculture and heavy manual work. Elsewhere there is a certain tendency for the occupational basis of the Jews to broaden gradually as access to all walks of life becomes open to them, but the tendency is, as might be expected, a slow one. About 2 per cent of Jews in the United States, for example, have taken to farming. But among Jews, as among all other western peoples, the tendency of the son is either to follow in the social grade, if not the actual profession, of his father, or to seek to rise to a higher grade. This rule has been found to hold good of immigrants (non-Jewish as well as Jewish) as much as of any other section of the population, and explains why, in countries where there are no restrictions, Jewish immigrants from Tsarist Russia tend to concentrate into the few occupations which they followed in the limited life, and primitive economy, of the country they had left behind. In the countries of the west, European or American Jews thus tend to show the same kind of social distribution that they showed in eastern Europe.

Among the professions the most popular in every country are law and medicine. For this one reason has already been given. Unlike the army or civil service, they were everywhere *free* professions, in which a man could make his way by his own personality and talents; and they thus attracted Jews in countries where access to government employment was impossible or extremely difficult. But they were also professions to which Jews took easily. The intense intellectual life of Jewry in the days when nearly all Jews were "orthodox" and students of the Talmud, was a good preparation for the subtleties of the law; while medicine was a profession they had practised in the days when their Christian fellow-practitioners still dealt in every kind of spell and superstition. It was a common practice of medieval princes, when they expelled their Jewish subjects, to make an exception of their own doctors! Jews are not only numerous among doctors, they are also prominent in every field of medical research, and no Nazi argument is more foolish than that which pretends that their number in the profession automatically implies a loss to medicine. Jewish names are to be found among the greatest in every field of modern medicine, including psychotherapy.

After medicine and law, the profession with which Jews are most popularly associated is that of finance—some perhaps would rank it first. Jewish association with finance goes back only to the Middle Ages, and the licensed usurer of the medieval prince. The Biblical promise that Israel should "lend unto many nations but should not borrow" does not refer to the modern type of international loans! It is a promise of prosperity among the mixed population of Palestine—the Jew would not have to borrow a pruning hook from his Philistine neighbor, he would have a spare one to lend him. A medieval background was, however, enough to give the Jew a good start in the immense commercial expansion of the 19th century; and the factor already referred to (p. 103) encouraged Jews to be among the more adventurous speculators and entrepreneurs of the period. In this they were helped by the fact that Jewish history had tended to make Jews more adventurous with their money than the ordinary man. The Christian tends to desire to save what he has obtained, because it gives him a certain security. If he makes enough money he can buy land and even found a landowning family. To Jews historically, the possession of money never meant security—and this has again been true in Europe since 1933—so that they risk it more easily for what it may produce today and tomorrow. It is, of course, true that the result of this adventurous and speculative spirit has been a number of Jewish financial crashes and scandals, and that in them non-Jews have often lost money. But it is equally true that Jewish initiative and imagination has been responsible for many developments in social and economic life. The now almost extinct "sweat-shops" of Jewish tailors of the East End of London have already been referred to; but what is more significant is the solid achievement of Jewish tailoring which is involved in putting well made and well cut clothes within the reach of all sections of the population, men and women. For almost the whole of that industry has been built up by Jewish energy. What is true of clothing is equally true in the furniture and catering trades. The hundreds of thousands of men and women with relatively low incomes who enjoy a meal and music, such as they would never otherwise have known, at the Lyons' Corner Houses owe their enjoyment to Jewish imagination.

The real characteristic of the Jewish community is not, however, the small number of great businesses on which antisemitic attention is concentrated. They are made to appear important only because of the general rule that Jews are concentrated into relatively few occupations. Such Jewish enterprises are not prominent in the general picture of "big business" in national life; in finance Jews are not prominent in the institutions which make financial policy—the great joint stock banks, the Bank of England and the Treasury; Jews are not found in heavy industry, mining or transport, which determine employment policies and the general picture of industrial life. The real characteristic of the Jewish community is the immense mass of little—often "one man"—businesses which take the place of the much more varied middle and lower-middle class occupations of non-Jewish national life. Skilled artisans and small shopkeepers, little family factories producing some specialized article—these are the real characteristics of Jewry, in pre-war Poland as much as in contemporary Leeds or New York. And it is here that, where there is truth in the charge, one form of Jewish "clannishness" sometimes appears. There are particular branches of special trades where Jews form an exceedingly high proportion of the whole. This came out in some of the studies made of the "black market." In one or two trades Jewish names appeared to fill a distressing proportion of the offenders—in one case over half. But an inquiry showed that in that particular trade not half but three-quarters of those engaged were Jews.* And, in defense of both Jews and non-Jews concerned, it can be added that the offenders altogether constituted a fraction of 1 per cent of those engaged in the trade.

A sociologist would find various reasons why a population thus narrowly distributed would be likely to draw exceptional and unfriendly attention to itself. It is in direct contact with the public without intermediaries. A paid employee will not be so readily blamed for what the buyer dislikes as the proprietor him- or herself. It is occupied with the trades in which varieties of price and price cutting are most possible—and this may incur the hostility of both buyers and competitors. It is also the section of commercial life in which men will vary most in the amount of personal effort they put into their work. An employee works for fixed hours. A shopkeeper can, if he desires it, often

---

*These facts are not "scientific," for the only bases of judgment were the names, and the personal knowledge of those making the inquiry. But the possible inaccuracy is not likely to modify the general picture.

increase his profits by working longer hours than his neighbors and competitors—and Jews are notoriously hard workers, who will thus be readily accused of taking away their living from those not prepared to work as long, or for such small profits, as they do. In some cases the sociologist would undoubtedly decide that the competition *was* unfair, and the unpopularity earned was merited. But in eastern Europe he would have found in innumerable cases that the Jewish shopkeeper could not hope to earn even the most miserable income by any other means. In western Europe he would as often see it as part of the continual conflict between consumer and producer in a capitalist economy, and estimate the distributor who, by his willingness to work for long hours or low profits, got the same goods to the public more cheaply than his competitor, actually to be performing a useful service.

Since the bulk of the Jewish community of every country is to be found among artisans and the lower-middle classes, he would soon find that the belief in the enormous wealth of the Jews was a myth. In eastern Europe the Jews were actually poorer than their Gentile neighbors since they were more dependent on a money economy, and on trade fluctuations and depression. The son or daughter of the peasant could go home and eat off the land; the son or daughter of the Jew could not. In the west he would probably decide that the reverse was true; the average Jewish income would tend to be a little higher than the national average, owing to the rarity of Jews among the lowest paid agricultural or unskilled urban workers. Nothing like comprehensive figures are available, and it would not be possible to obtain them, except in countries where the official census registers Jews as Jews. It would therefore remain an impression.

Statistics on "Jewish criminality" are likewise obtainable only in countries where sentences are recorded according to the religion of the offender. But while they may not constitute proof for the situation in countries where such statistics do not exist, they at least provide a fairly useful guide—unless it be supposed that the Jews are so subtle that they abstain from crime in one country and commit it in another after previous examination of the national method of recording public statistics! Attempts to sort out the actual facts of black market offenses in this country did not reveal any especial viciousness on the part of Jewish business men. They were usually proportionate to the number of Jewish firms in the trade examined, and sometimes even appeared less than might be expected. This question of proportion is really the key to the situation. Jews are more apt to be convicted of commercial offenses because proportionately they are more occupied with commerce than the rest of the community. They are more apt to be convicted of offenses such as one would associate with "foreigners" because, even when they are not of immediate foreign origin, an antisemitic environment saps the instinctive loyalty we expect of those whose membership of the community is never questioned. On the other hand, they are rarely convicted of crimes of brutality or violence—especially against children, and this reflects a high moral level of civilization in the community concerned, whatever its economic or occupational failings.

Politically their story is scarcely more interesting. Of the supposed unity, profundity and determination of the hypothetical "Elders of Zion" a sociologist would not find the slightest trace. The internal politics of Jewish communities are conspicuous for the violence of their divisions, and the unimportance (to an outside mind) of the issues on which the divisions are usually based. They are, in fact, exactly what our hypothetical sociologist would expect of their circumstances; and he would find plenty of parallels either from small town politics, or from the frustrations and bitternesses of groups which are not actually free to be masters of their own destiny. As to the political activities of Jews as individuals, they tend to reflect the political outlook of the class and country to which they belong. Wealthy Jews tend to be conservative, poor Jews to be socialist, in the same way as poor and wealthy members of the rest of society. In the 19th century the bulk of the Jewish vote would have been given to liberals of different shades, because it was liberalism which led to their emancipation. Today the distinction is blurred. In countries where they are oppressed, they will naturally contain a larger proportion of revolutionaries. But it is equally true that, in proportion to the numbers involved, Jewish members of the Left will be more noticeable than those of the Right. For those on the Right are less wealthy and socially prominent than the average leader of the Right, possessed perhaps of an ancient title, or belonging to an ancient family; but those on the Left are better educated and, in eastern Europe at least, often of quicker intelligence than the bulk of workers or peasants who make up the forces of the Left. It was this which made Jews—little more than a handful statistically—so prominent among the early leaders of the Communist revolution that the government of the U.S.S.R. and the Communist Party which kept it in power were quite commonly believed to be almost wholly Jewish.

At the time of writing (November, 1944) the activities of a small group of terrorists is much before the public eye because of the dastardly assassination of Lord Moyne. Terrorists are an almost unknown feature in the Jewish history of more than a thousand years, and even now probably number only a few hundred.

Numerically, occupationally, economically and politically, there is really nothing remarkable about the
Jewries of the world. There is no field in which a
sociologist would find himself confronted with situations which were a national menace.

No study of the Jewish community would, of course,
be complete which took no account of the synagogue.
Individually Jews may attend worship as little as Christians, but the religion of the synagogue has created the
pattern of their lives as much as Roman Catholicism,
Orthodoxy, or Protestantism have molded different
sections of European civilization.

Two thousand years ago, before the coming of Christianity, Julius Cæsar gave extensive privileges to the
Jewish communities of the Roman Empire because he
had decided that Judaism made good citizens. The
Empires of the Nile and Euphrates valleys did the
same. More, they used Jewish soldiers to guard their
most dangerous frontiers, beeause they found them especially reliable. In the Middle Ages the princes and
the church permitted Jews to practise usury because
they considered it was permitted by the Jewish religion (actually they were wrong; and based their view
on a mistranslation), but the medieval public went to
Jewish usurers because they found them more honest
than the Christian. Beneath all the froth and scum created by modern antisemitism, and after taking into account all the qualifications, due to history and environment, already discussed, it is still true that the evidence
from all countries is that Judaism makes of its adher-
ents good citizens.

The first interesting feature of Judaism is that after
the loss of Palestine it did not meet the dispersion and
persecution of its people with a religion of comfort,
resignation and escape. It is true that in eastern Europe
in the 19th century and in corners of England or Amer-

ica today, there are to be found Jews living a life apart from the bustle of everyday activity, and wrapped in Talmudic argument or mystical speculation. But the characteristic of Judaism is activity. When independence was finally lost after the disastrous wars with Rome, the religious leaders set out to make their religion a "portable home" for the Jewish people. On the one hand they emphasized those ritual and ceremonial loyalties which "made a hedge about the Law," and kept the whole significance of Jewish life clear-cut and distinct. On the other they insisted that the "righteousness of God" would be vindicated in this world, and that Jews must so live that the name of God would be honored. While Judaism accepts life after death, there is no tendency to make a future life iron out the inequalities of this one. In every generation the rabbis emphasized that righteousness is to be sought for here and now. The blending of ethical and ritual teaching into a single whole would appeal to a modern psychologist who knows how much our daily actions count in our total make-up, and how small the value of moral generalizations can be.

The second characteristic is its tremendous interest in questions which the ordinary Christian would not consider to be specifically 'religious.' There are to be found in the Talmud and in rabbinical writings of all centuries, discussions of education, courts of justice, laws of evidence, laws of contract, and all sorts of economic and cultural questions—but it must be added that rabbinical writings are extremely difficult to understand, and apparently filled with extraordinarily unimportant details. They are not secret, but they are obscure.

The third characteristic is its democracy. The Jewish world has an 'aristocracy' consisting of the Spanish or Sephardic Jews; but Judaism has no conception of authority of interpretation other than the moral authority of the interpreters, except on matters of ceremonial. Judaism has no popes or bishops; and worship is 'congregational.' The rabbi is not a priest.

Finally there is its optimism. Judaism is throughout an optimistic religion. It is not a superficial optimism, and it is balanced by the fact—or rests on the fact—that the one day of the year which is observed by nearly all Jews is the Day of Atonement, the day of self-examination and spiritual "stock-taking" as well as penitence.

There are, of course, many other points in Judaism which are significant; there are types of Jewish piety and mysticism to fascinate the student of religion, but in so far as Judaism is intimately related to the pattern of Jewish life, it is these which are, perhaps, the more important. Finally, it must be emphasized that there is nothing *secret* in Judaism. The usual antisemitic charges of secret practices, of double meanings, of ritual concealed from Gentile observers and so on, rest only on their own imaginations. Nor need this be accepted on the word of Jewish authorities only—Jewish books have been too often confiscated by Christian censors, Jewish activities too often scrutinized by hostile examiners familiar with Hebrew, too many reputable Jews have become converts to Christianity, for sinister practices to have been kept secret by a people so dispersed for centuries among a non-Jewish population.

It is only as we get entirely away from the kind of matters which the antisemite proclaims to be characteristic of the Jewish community that the sociologist would reach those aspects of it which actually cause friction. But one difficulty must be frankly faced. Those spheres in which real friction arises are spheres in which it is impossible to obtain statistical data and judgment founded on completely objective scientific observation.

Many good examples of this fact and of the scale of the real problem are to be found in the field of education. Those whose business it is to examine for entrance to the universities are confronted with the fact that Jewish boys or girls tend to mature more quickly than others. It may be that insecurity tends to encourage early maturity; for it is noticeable that the children of the poor are often older for their age than the sheltered children of the rich. It may be that the traditional respect for the intellect in a Jewish household encourages precocity in the children. It was certainly true in Poland that the young Jew learned more easily than the son of the peasant. It may even be that there are some people who mature more rapidly than others. There has not been adequate research to give us an answer; but the fact remains one of observation, if not of scientific proof; the Jewish child matures more quickly. Between 20 and 23 the differences even out, but at the age of matriculation and scholarship examinations, the Jew is likely to appear ahead of the non-Jew who may be his equal or surpass him a few years later. The university examiner has to try to judge which of two candidates will really go further. It is easy, if he decide against the Jew, for a Jewish home to be embittered with the feeling that it has been discriminated against. It is equally easy for a Gentile home, if the Jew gets the place, to feel jealousy and bitterness. No one could pretend that a threat to national life was involved either way. But it is a threat to the happiness, and perhaps the economic wellbeing, of two families, and it is of such stuff that local feeling grows.

It might not be possible to prove that Jews, as a community, were more intellectual than others, for scientific tests would not be easy to apply; but an observer would find a number of differences in the general field of intellect, some of which provoke trouble, some of which do not. It is, for example, the rarest thing to find a Jewish home in which the things of the intellect are despised; but I do not know of any way in which this could produce ill-feeling. On the other hand the Jewish delight in argument, often argument for its own sake, can irritate the more phlegmatic—or dogmatic—of their neighbors. But the difference does not merely consist in the Jewish love of an argument. In the argument itself Jews will tend to stress, and attach importance to, points which most non-Jews would relegate to a much less prominent place. Legality seems to them much more important than practicality; formal rights than 'fair-play'; logical justification than common sense. Here we touch on differences which may rise to the fringe of national issues. Much of the bitterness of Zionist argument with the British about the fulfilment of the Palestine Mandate, much of the general Jewish indignation against the Polish or Hungarian authorities in the years before 1939 over the limitation of Jewish access to the universities, arose from this difference of standpoint, entirely apart from whether the case itself was a good one or not. In both cases it was difficult for Jews to see beyond the infringement, or non-fulfilment, of formal rights. No student of Jewish history would find any difficulty in understanding these Jewish emphases. For many centuries Jews owed their rights of residence, and their economic and social wellbeing, to precise privileges, formally negotiated, whose observance was a matter of life or death to the Jews involved. Peoples who dwell in their own territories have no such background; their rights rest on no such formal and legal basis; they have grown up by centuries of give and take, and slowly expanding liberties. But it is not only history which creates the differences in this field; the difference in religion has also made its contribution. Judaism approves of argument.

Although there are profound differences in the nature and structure of Judaism and Christianity, in the majority of cases these play no part in the creation of popular feeling. But the intensely democratic nature of Judaism, in which religious argument of the freest kind has a prominent place even in the traditional use of the synagogue, naturally creates a temperament different from that created by the Christian tradition, where authority is much more prominent, and where the very idea of arguing in church seems irreverent. As another example of the way in which religion affects the situation, we can see that there is nothing in the Jewish conception of the Sabbath which could create ill-feeling. But the fact that it is celebrated on a different day from the usual day of rest in the non-Jewish community can create trouble especially in districts which are half residential, half commercial.

A combination of religion and history accounts for another feature which exists in any Jewish community. and which, as soon as it attracts unfavorable attention, is labelled clannishness. The Jewish religion lays immense emphasis on the community, and on the mutual responsibility of members for each other. The overflowing of Jewish charity to all kinds of non-Jewish hospitals and social purposes shows the depth of this feeling among Jews; and it is natural that as soon as there is persecution or distress in any part of the Jewish world, Jews everywhere will forget their differences in the provision of succor. In itself this activity can arouse no hostility—if it does it is based on an unworthy jealousy or selfishness. But Jewish history comes in to complicate the matter. In their insecurity Jews are so often dependent on the help and support of their coreligionists that it is natural that a Jew who has found his own feet should turn to help others to the security he has found for himself, and this helps to intensify Jewish concentration, geographically, socially and economically. The statement that once a Jew is established anywhere he will bring in all his relations, is sometimes true; that a Jew will help his coreligionists in business to the exclusion of non-Jews is also sometimes true. That the reverse is also often true is of no importance in combatting the charge of clannishness. It is ruled out by the considerations governing minorities already discussed (p. 88). While this 'clannishness' may cause a real local problem in commercial or social life, it can create a fictitious problem in much more serious circumstances. In times of economic depression and unemployment, when it is easy to stir up enmity against any 'foreign' group, the belief that the 'foreigners' in question all hang together in order to deprive the 'native' of work may provide a fertile breeding ground for political antisemitism. And in times of international insecurity it is the breeding ground whence grow beliefs in international plots and maneuvers.

At various points the difficulties arising from a relatively recent foreign origin have already been discussed. Many habits which popular opinion hold to be 'Jewish' would be found by an observer simply to be normal habits of other countries. Since the bulk of western Jewry are descended from refugees who fled from Russia in the last sixty years, and since the smaller but not less significant group of refugees from Nazi Europe have appeared only in the last dozen years, it is to be expected that many foreign customs would survive among them. One important matter, that of the instinctive attitude to laws of those who came from Tsarist Russia, has already been discussed (p. 100), but there are many others.

One of the explanations given of the apparent early maturing of Jewish adolescents is that it is biological in origin. Without indulging in fantastic theories of race, it is possible to recognize that the physical heredity of the Jewish community is different from that of, for example, the Anglo-Saxon; and that the consequence is a general difference of physical characteristics. Some people appear to find these physical differences unpleasant or even repulsive; and, where this is the case, there is nothing much to be done. The feeling is subjective and irrational, and is probably a rationalization of quite different emotions. But even where the feeling of repulsion does not exist, characteristics are attributed to unalterable racial inheritances which in fact are the observable products of history and environment in other countries.

One source of friction is the dislike of the flashy dress and ostentatious behavior observable among Jews, which is attributed to their being 'orientals.' In physical heredity Jews are not a scrap more oriental than the majority of other Europeans. Part of the origin of this habit—where it exists—is probably the Jewish tendency to spend rather than save money, to which reference has already been made. But in the main it is simply the carry-over of a general continental custom. The Englishman and woman are as universally considered on the continent to be slipshod in dress as the Jews are considered to be flashy in dress in England. I remember being almost embarrassed once when chairing a student conference on the continent to find myself wearing flannels and an open shirt, when most of those continentals who intended to speak had arrayed themselves in stiff collars, black coats and striped trousers. But if this habit survives a generation or two after their arrival, that is as long as it does; for anyone who is familiar with the older Anglo-Jewish families will find them as devoted to their simple costumes, their ancient flannel trousers, and their comfortable tweed suits as any other members of the British middle-class.

There are other continental habits which have caused comment, particularly about the recent refugees from Nazi Europe. Late and noisy parties, elaborate entertainments and receptions, sun-bathing on the front lawn (until they discover that at least the Englishman knows his own climate), bargaining in shops or treating shopping as a long and argumentative process, an un-English treatment of officials and employees, lack of spontaneous and voluntary discipline in queues and such like—all these things are not 'Jewish,' for they are not to be observed in established Anglo-Jewish families. They are continental habits, which take some time to wear off. But they can cause local irritation. In one particular case war circumstances created quite a serious feeling of hostility. Many refugees were unemployed owing to the restrictions on the employment of aliens at the beginning of the war. Having nothing to do they were able to take their places early in queues; having time on their hands they could argue with shopkeepers; not having achieved our voluntary discipline, they resented any criticism of this behavior —and the result was just what might be expected. But I am reminded of a half-humorous conversation with a distinguished professor of the Sorbonne, not a Jew, who defined for me the idea of liberty in France: "Every day I come by the Métro; there is a notice 'passage forbidden,' and I pass. It is written up 'No spitting,' and I spit. And I am a professor of the Sorbonne! That is our liberty." He would cause considerable comment in England.

It is because people observe such things in their own actual environment that they lend an ear to antisemitic falsifications, which appear to be merely the extension of these observable matters to a wider field. It is no wonder that many real friends cry in despair: "Why doesn't the Jewish community do something about it?" A brutal answer is: "Why should they?" For, as has already been said, one would not dream of asking the Archbishop of Canterbury to stop racing touts on the grounds that they had been baptized in the Church of England. A more sensible answer is that many of such matters time will solve, and to make them the subject of official action is just psychologically wrong, and stirs up all the wrong reactions in Jews— in exactly the same way as it would in non-Jews. If I moderate my radio out of deference to my neighbor, that is because of my personal relations with him, not because he has asked the Vicar to come round and talk to me about it. If he does that, I am more likely to tell the Vicar this is a free country, and he can go—wherever Vicars do go! I then turn the radio on twice as loud, knowing that this is just not loud enough to bring serious reprisals from the local police. Is not this how most of the world would act? And why can we not realize Jews react in just the same way? Of course, some Jews really enjoy being nasty, and some non-Jews may have the misfortune to have such among their neighbors. But so, in my experience, do some Englishmen, Frenchmen, Czechs, Americans, and— had I lived in their countries also, I should doubtless be able to add—Hottentots, Singhalese, Dutch and Eskimos. The basic trouble is that we have become so "Jew-conscious" that we lose all sense of proportion in dealing with any question which affects the Jews.

If much of our basic trouble is that we have become artificially "Jew-conscious" the basic trouble on the

Jewish side is that *they have suffered too much from the antisemitism bred and spread by Nazi Germany to be able to react normally to our criticisms.* For the deepest and saddest conclusion to which our sociologist would come after his study of the Jewish community is that it is a community suffering from an intolerable nervous exhaustion. We know that though there is no 'international Jewish conspiracy' yet nearly every Jewish family has close relations in other countries—often parents, sons and daughters, brothers and sisters, not just distant cousins. For five years they have lived under the strain of knowing that these nearest relatives may not only be dead, but may have been done to death with every refinement of torture; yes, or may be still alive enduring a life that is worse than death. And while others have done this to them, they are expected to behave with impeccable table-manners to others, to take official action at the slightest offense committed by one of their members, to accept responsibility for all their black sheep in a way in which we would not dream of taking responsibility for our own, and to be profoundly grateful if we show any understanding of their situation, and pass a resolution of sympathy with their misfortunes, unaccompanied by any action to alleviate them.

For a hundred pages I have been trying to dissect analytically, coldly, and objectively "the Jewish problem." I have done it without more regard to the feelings of my Jewish friends than a surgeon can have of the patient under his knife. It had to be done so, or it would have had no value. But before I go on to discuss, equally objectively, what we are to do about it, will the non-Jewish reader pardon me this explosion? Put yourself for a moment in the place of the Jews. Imagine you know that your mother has died of starvation in a Polish forest; that your sister has been violated in a Nazi brothel in Belgium; that your young nephews have been thrown into an oven in a French torture camp, because you could not get for them in time certificates from the British administration to admit them to Palestine; and that you have heard nothing for five years of your brother—whether he be alive or dead—and then imagine you have to sit in the suburban train and listen to your neighbors abusing "Jew boys," analyzing your manners, exaggerating all your faults, maliciously distorting your sorrows, and accusing you of every crime envy and ignorance could devise. Well? Would the crime rate remain low in your vicinity? Would there be no hesitation about your loyalty? Would you be tempted to no antisocial act or feeling? Well?

CHAPTER VII

THE ELIMINATION OF ANTISEMITISM

THE first and most essential thing to be said about the elimination of antisemitism is that the first two steps to be taken—steps without which most of what follows would be sterile—have nothing to do with antisemitism. So long as the world is a place in which life to the ordinary man means insecurity, frustration and unemployment, so long will he need some scapegoat for his feelings; and the position of the Jews, and their powerlessness, make them the perfect scapegoat. Human nature is conservative; men have been accustomed to blame the Jews, and it will be easier to change the world into a pleasant place to live in than to leave it as it is, and expect them to find another scapegoat. This is not meant flippantly. The world had been made so "Jew-conscious" by Nazi propaganda; men have been taught so sedulously to associate the Jews with all their miseries, frustrations and bitternesses, that no amount of deliberate education would eliminate those associations, while their grievances are left unremedied. The cure of antisemitism is intimately bound up with the solution of our national and social problems.

The second essential is complementary to the first. It is impossible to cure antisemitism while the situation of the Jews remains as it is. While it is true that a small minority of the Jewish people has become completely absorbed, by generations of slow and easy assimilation, into the life surrounding them, the immense majority of those Jews who survive this war will be dominated by a sense of utter insecurity; they will remain a hypersensitive, unadaptable, psychologically unbalanced, nervous irritant in the body politic, easy game for the unscrupulous propagandist, until conditions are created for them in which they can really feel secure. I say "conditions created for them" deliberately; for the Jews are everywhere powerless to determine the conditions of their own existence. Even where they 'enjoy complete equality' with the rest of the population, they do so by the good will of that population. And that is not complete equality. This might have seemed an overstatement fifteen years ago; but no Jew can forget the experience of the ancient and well-assimilated communities of Germany, of Italy and of France under Nazi domination, or ignore the warning that it was the mistakes of Germany in not attacking England in June, 1940, or Syria in June, 1941, rather than the strength of Great Britain, which preserved the Jewries of Palestine, England, and perhaps the rest of the world from a similar fate. This fact relates the second essential to the first. For just as the ordinary man will not relinquish his accustomed scapegoat while he remains economically and politically insecure; so the Jew will not relax his anxiety so long as he fears the menace of war hanging over the world. If this were all that was contained in the second step, then the first two conditions would be merely the obverse and reverse of the same picture. But it is not all. More is needed than merely the absence of war or of economic and social tension. The Jewish situation in 1939 was abnormal and unsatisfactory; and it definitely needs to be one of the matters dealt with in any congress dealing with the reconstruction of the world.

That congress will have to deal with two situations—

that of the National Home, and that of the Jews of the European continent west of the Soviet border, including those who are temporarily refugees elsewhere. The Palestinian situation cannot rightly be discussed merely on the basis of continuing or discontinuing the solution offered at the end of the First World war. A re-examination is needed on the basis of the position today. Likewise in Europe more is required than merely the re-establishment of the *status quo* of before 1933 or 1939.

However controversial the Palestinian question may be it cannot be dodged. Jewish interest in the country is not merely sentimental; either Palestine is made capable of fulfilling the needs of a large number of Jews, or the world has not only got to find some other place which will house a Jewish community of a million or more—which so far it has completely failed to do—but it has also to find several hundred million pounds to replace the work done already in Palestine.

Nothing is gained by misrepresenting the facts about Palestine from either side. The Jewish claim to make their home in the country rests on three foundations, and the claim itself is the most important factor in the psychological situation of contemporary Jewry. Many hundreds of thousands of Jews (before the massacres of 1941-45 one could have said several million) feel themselves to be a people as much as any other people in the world, and desire to lead their own life, not as a minority among others, but in a country of their own; and this desire centers in their ancient homeland, where more than half a million of them have already settled, not just in any uninhabited corner of the world. Secondly, the legitimacy of this desire was recognized by the League of Nations which established the Palestine Mandate. Thirdly, some further tens—probably hundreds—of thousands of Jews are homeless; they do not desire to return to lands which have become a nightmare to them, and the world has so far found them nowhere else to go.

It is false to oppose to this Jewish position either the idea that it automatically overrides the rights of the Arabs, or, on the other hand, a conception of an Arab Palestine, fully populated by the ancestors of the present Arab population for a period of centuries and millenia. The frontiers created in 1919 are quite new and artificial frontiers; they do not correspond to any historic Turkish or Arab divisions. They were created to divide the British and French Mandates, roughly along the line of the Biblical frontier of the Holy Land. Historically Palestine is part of "Syria," and the Arabs of Palestine are Syrians. Considerably more than half of those living at present in Palestine originally lived, or are descended from Arabs who lived, in the northern part of Syria or in other Arab countries, until the prosperity consequent on Zionist colonization gradually drew them by the prospect of work and high wages. Very many Arabs have actually entered the country since 1920. What the League of Nations did, from the historical standpoint, was to divide Syria and create favored conditions for Jewish immigration in the southern, and then less populated, portion. The making of Palestine (or part of it) into a Jewish Commonwealth would not be destroying an Arab country; it would be diminishing the area of Syria.

The right of the Jews is genuinely but, from an exclusively political point of view somewhat weakly, based on ancient association and residence; but strongly based on a valid international decision. The right of the Arabs is also less strongly based on past association than pro-Arab propaganda claims, but strongly based on the actual fact that they are as legitimately living in Palestine as I am in England. On both sides I have omitted the promises made during the 1914 war, which present an interesting tangle for the historian and the lawyer, but offer no guidance for the practical consideration of the future. This is especially so as the contradictions in them are the responsibility neither of the Jews nor of the Arabs.

Many who espouse the Arab case think to strengthen their position by denouncing the right of the League of Nations to have embodied the promises made to the Jews (the Balfour Declaration) in a Mandate under its authority. They refuse to see the possibility of an equal validity being attributed to a 'natural' right and a right explicitly created by an international decision; and they appear to regard the latter as a unique and quite unparalleled action. It is quite legitimate to consider it a wrong decision, but not on that basis. Unless we accept an entirely static conception of the world, we must recognize that conditions have, from time to time, to be changed, and that the right way for them to be changed, when it is not the result of mutual negotiation and consent, is for it to be done after full consideration by the highest constituted authority; and we recognize that this authority has the right and duty to act, even when the persons concerned do not consent. The same thing is done by our own and other Parliaments and local councils in internal matters—as, for example, when the recognized authority sanctions the dispossession of farmers in a valley to make a reservoir for a city. It was done internationally after the last war in the exchange of populations between Greece and Turkey, and in various plebiscites and disputed areas; and it has often been done before. Naturally it should be reserved for exceptional situations, and should not be done except for good and valid reason; and the real question with which we are confronted is: had the League of Nations (which was the properly constituted authority at the time) good and valid reason for deciding that in southern Syria the normal rights of the Arabs should be interfered with to the advantage of the Jews? In making our judgment we can legitimately take into account the general underpopulation of all the Arab countries, so that there would certainly be room elsewhere for Arabs who might find it intolerable to live under Jewish rule; but I doubt if we should judge on the basis of various acts of Arab disloyalty to the United Nations during the war. We should take into account the desperate Jewish need of some place of security somewhere, and the facts both that the world has failed to provide it elsewhere, and that no other country can have the same appeal for Jews as Palestine; but, again I doubt if we should judge on the basis of the war service in all the Mediterranean and African fronts of Jewish soldiers from Palestine.

On this quite unemotional basis, a basis primarily of need, I believe that the League of Nations was right in its decision. Today we are confronted with a further problem. The Jewish National Home is now a vigorous body with over half a million members which has performed miracles in the restoration of fertility and activity to the country. It has reached the point where it is, in itself, ripe for transformation into a Jewish Commonwealth, and the Mandate was always intended to be temporary. Is the next stage to be a bi-national state, shared with the Arab population? This is what the original Mandate envisaged, and on paper this would be the easiest solution, involving the least friction or dispossession of any existing rights. But all the evidence is that it would not work. It is, as has been said, yoking together two horses, one of which cannot stop and the other of which does not wish to start. The Arabs have shown complete unwillingness to accept the pace or further growth of the Jewish community. It is more important to recognize the fact than to blame them for it. It is, in fact, very easy to understand their opposition. But from a practical point of view this attitude of the Arabs makes the alternatives either the abandonment of the idea of building a National Home, or the decision to transfer political authority to it.

I wish the necessity for such a decision had not arisen. I wish the Jews and Arabs had been able to "dwell together in amity." I wish the Jews were more sensible politicians. I wish the Arabs were less liable to be carried away by extremism. I wish all sorts of things. But they won't alter the actual situation. In southern Syria conditions exist in which two rights confront each other, both valid; two desires confront each other, both legitimate, both entitled to our consideration. But they are in conflict, and the world is called to decide between them on a practical basis. The right basis seems to me that of supporting the greater need; of inflicting the lesser hardship.

I believe that the Jewish case wins by this test; and that Palestine should become a Jewish Commonwealth. The actual area to be thus cut from Syria need not necessarily correspond exactly to the frontiers of 1919. But they should not be very much less. For the Jordan Valley is a unity capable of development along the lines of the "Tennessee Valley Authority" and useless to both parties if it is divided.

If such a Jewish Commonwealth were to be established, then the second aspect of the question, the situation of the Jews in Europe, is not difficult of solution. For there is a home to which those who do not wish to remain in Europe are able to go. So far as Europe itself is concerned there are two essentials: that the full legal equality which existed in 1939 should be restored, and there is little doubt that this will be done in western Europe; and that there should be no compulsion on those who have been driven from their countries and deprived of citizenship, to return if they do not wish to. It is right to cancel the acts of the German government since 1933; it is wrong to deduce from this that those Jews who were German citizens in 1933, and who are now stateless, should be compelled to return to Germany. As to eastern Europe the situation is still obscure. No one knows what will be the number of the survivors or their desires. But it seems probable that the solution in western Europe—individual equality— will be adequate. There will no longer be numbers such as would warrant the re-establishment of the Minority Treaties. But here the first condition indicated in this chapter is of evident importance. The formal grant of individual equality will not secure justice, if eastern Europe is to return to the poverty, the fascist politics and the instability of the inter-war years. Only if there is a real change in the situation will life be tolerable for the Jews or any other minority group.

If the Jews were exactly the same as any other minority one might almost end there. We have seen that there are certain disabilities a minority must suffer from, but that it is only when there is insecurity and frustration among the majority that these disabilities are likely to be intolerable. In normal and prosperous times they are not an impossible price to pay for the privilege—fact—liability—whatever one may call it—of desiring to remain permanently an identifiable minority. But the Jews are not like any other minority. There are in fact minorities which cause locally much more acute problems than the Jews—the gypsies in Europe, the nomads in the Arab lands, the Chinese in Siam, the Japanese on the Pacific Coast of America, and so on. But the world is not gypsy-conscious or nomad-conscious—or even Chinese- or Japanese-conscious. Whereas it is "Jew-conscious." If I were asked what

proportion of the population were at least slightly unbalanced on the subject of the Jews, I would say: about
95 per cent, including all the Jews themselves, and all
the people who have made a deep study of the Jewish
question. And I do not intend the 5 per cent I have
omitted to represent the most intelligent section of the
community. The assassination of Lord Moyne provided
two excellent examples of this peculiarity. A leader in
The Times on November 10, 1944, entitled *A Call to
Jewry,* made the following remark about the acceptance of responsibility for hunting down the assassins
by all the Jewish community of Palestine:

> "The Jews have been the principal victims of the
> Nazi doctrine of the glorification of violence and, as
> such, have won the eager sympathy of men of good
> will throughout the world. They would stand to lose
> all if they seemed to become in the least degree con-
> taminated by the villainies from which they have
> suffered."

Now this is sheer nonsense; and, if it were dealing with
any other subject, *The Times* would realize it was sheer
nonsense. *All* human beings who have been through
great sufferings are 'contaminated' by them. And yet
The Times warns that they will forfeit all sympathy—
not *some* sympathy, mark you, but *all* sympathy—with
their sufferings if the unfortunate Jews even "seems to
be" contaminated. And a few days later, on November
17, in the House of Commons Mr. Churchill himself,
who has always been a chivalrous friend of the National Home, solemnly announced that the existence of
a small band of terrorists would make many like himself "reconsider the position we have maintained so
consistently and so long in the past"; and he ended by
demanding that "every man, woman and child of the

140

Jewish community" should do "his or her best to bring this terrorism to a speedy end." Terrorists are an unpleasant phenomenon. They should certainly be got rid of. But they are not a phenomenon that we usually invite women and children to hunt out! Nor do people, when they are sane, announce that they will change their views about a project in which hundreds of thousands of honest men have been engaged for several generations because for a brief period a band, which probably does not number a couple of hundred, breaks down under a strain they have found intolerable and takes to the folly of assassination. We are indeed all slightly mad on the Jewish question! In no field has Hitler's propaganda been more successful; in no other field could it claim *The Times* leader writer and the Prime Minister among its victims.

And it is the same with us ordinary folk. We believe stories about the Jews; we see a menace in activities of the Jews; we argue about the Jews; in a way we would do about no other folk. It is not that we are cruel or malicious. But we have been thoroughly bedevilled. It is a good to remember that Hitler says openly in *Mein Kampf* that a lie will be believed provided it is a big enough lie and repeated often enough. The Nazis knew quite well what they were doing when they started their anti-Jewish propaganda. Our attitude to our Jewish neighbors is evidence of the truth of Hitler's statement, and of the success of its application.

In consequence of this peculiarity we have got to go further. We cannot leave it at the two points already mentioned. In some way or another we have got to make a direct attack on the menace of antisemitism— we have got to recover our sanity and kindness. The first point is to realize that it is primarily not a problem for Jews to deal with. They cannot hope to succeed, for the most visible symptom of the disease they are fighting is that its victims do not believe anything that Jews say. It is we, the majority, who catch the disease, and it is for us to find the treatment. Of course, *pace The Times* Jews are also "contaminated" by it; but we will deal with that in a minute.

Many people say that the first thing to do is to make the propagation of antisemitism illegal; that is, pass a law against "community libel." Legal proceedings have been taken in many countries; and, unfortunately, the evidence from those countries is not very encouraging. In Republican Germany many Nazi leaders were brought into court, tried and convicted for blasphemy on various occasions before 1933! They found the court proceedings a rather valuable platform for making antisemitic utterances, and that any fines they paid were well spent. If the punishments are not very severe they will not stop the offense; if they are savage, they will turn the convicted offender into a martyr. Those are the disadvantages. In the Soviet Union such a law also existed, and had no such disadvantages; but that is because it was part of a whole campaign, and not the most important part. For the attack on antisemitism took place on a basis of increasing security and employment; in other words, the general situation was favorable. Moreover the center of the campaign was education in racial tolerance within the proletarian society, and antisemitism was pilloried or 'bourgeois' and 'reactionary,' which was much more serious than just making it 'illegal.' Legislation might be a useful adjunct in a general campaign; it cannot take the place of other methods of dealing with the disease, or even occupy the central position among other methods. It certainly could not be of the slightest value if we are not at the same time tackling the removal of insecurity and frustration from the lives of ordinary men, and from the Jewish community.

It is more valuable to make fascist propaganda unattractive than to make it illegal. Openly fascist bodies will, doubtless, be proscribed in many countries; but crypto-fascism can be just as dangerous. From the purely legal point of view the prohibition of uniforms, of para-military parades and organizations, and of secrecy in finance, would be legitimate measures, and possibly do more than direct prohibition of community libel. They cut a little nearer the source of the evil. But the main emphasis must be on education.

Here the Soviet example is of great value. They did more by making the exhibition of racial prejudice something to be ashamed of than by making it something to be punished. And this raises another issue. A country like the U.S.A. is gravely impeded in an attempt to remove prejudice against the Jew, so long as it overlooks serious prejudice against the Negro; and the same is true in South Africa. For racial prejudice, like peace, is indivisible. Here in England that side of the matter presents fewer difficulties; and a great deal could be done in schools and political organizations to spread information and to attack ignorance. But we shall, unfortunately, have to do it without being able to attach the magnificently derogatory word "bourgeois" to it! But, on the other hand, we can quite honestly point out its use by the Nazis, and present it as part of the Nazi attack on democracy in our own and other countries. And the progressives at any rate can show how often it is used by selfish reactionary interests as a smokescreen to cover their own activities.

Side by side with the approach to the subject within the orbit of a larger curriculum, whether of school or of political organization, it is possible to approach the subject directly in organizations of local Jews and Christians, or even committees of Jews and Christians attached to other local bodies in areas in which numbers of Jews reside, and where local feeling may be dangerous and local knowledge will certainly be useful. It is in the work of such societies or committees that we come to the Jewish side of the matter. Two of the consequences—inevitable but lamentable—of the present general neurosis about the Jews, coming on top of the appalling horror of the massacre of several million Jews in Nazi death camps, is that really kindly and sensitive men and women feel as unable to criticize what ought to be criticized in the life or conduct of individual Jews or of the Jewish community they know, as they would be unable to criticize the business conduct of a friend on the day of the death of his wife. And the Jews on their side, battered and humiliated by a thousand accusations which they know to be false, mourning for the martyrdom of their brethren under Nazi rule, and fearful to make the slightest admission which could be turned to their disadvantage, resent as antisemitic the gentlest suggestion, and wrap themselves in a perfection which never was on land or sea. Only as the tensity of the atmosphere begins to relax under the healing rays of friendship, co-operation and knowledge, is constructive work capable of being done.

The main difficulty in such societies is that there are not enough non-Jews who know anything about Jewish history or the actual facts of contemporary Jewish life. They should not always depend for their information on Jews; for there are situations in which non-Jews need to be left to discuss the question by themselves. Apart from the particular tensions of the present moment, there is a natural reluctance among decent people to criticize a man to his face; and only too often the real sentiments and beliefs of a group of non-Jews are expressed when the Jewish colleagues with whom they have been discussing things have left the room. And it can be disastrous if there is no non-Jew left who knows anything about the question. In every community in which there is a local Jewish population it ought to be the duty of a local society of Jews and Christians to see that in the municipal offices and among the municipal councillors and committees; in the educational committees, among the magistrates and police; and among the local churches there are some non-Jews who know something solid about the Jewish question.*

A particular responsibility lies upon the churches. And, with many notable exceptions, their ignorance is both dishonorable and disgusting. There is nothing whatever to be said in their defense. They maintain missions to convert the Jews, while at the same time they will not spend a penny of either time or effort to see that Judaism and the story of the Jewish people are fairly presented to their congregations. This might not matter if they could ignore the Jews. But references to them are bound to crop up continually in sermons, lectures and books; and nine-tenths of those references are ill-informed, often to the point of being definitely untrue. They don't mean to be prejudiced; they are not conscious of antisemitic feeling; but the share that they bear for providing a fertile breeding ground for every kind of antisemitic misrepresentation is an exceedingly heavy one; and a few resolutions of sympathy with the victims of Hitler's massacres do not square the account. Innumerable ministers of religion preach sermons on the Pharisees; and know nothing whatever about them. They talk of "the Law" and they have not the slightest idea what "Torah" (the Hebrew for Law) means to a Jew. They speak of "the Jews" when they describe the less attractive activities of the early Israelites with complete indifference to the fact that the congregation will relate

*See Bibliography No. 2 at end.

their words to the conduct of a contemporary 20th-century Jewish community. This is particularly the case in their ignorant contrasts of the 'Jewish' and 'Christian' ideas of God. I have met ministers who believed that "love thy neighbor as thyself" was an entirely New Testament idea, and are unaware that Jesus is endorsing the teaching of Moses (Lev. xix. 18), not giving original teaching Himself in the passage. With sublime indifference to the evidence of the Synoptic Gospels themselves (which contain no mention of the Pharisees in the events of the arrest, trial and death of Jesus), they lay the blame for the Crucifixion on Pharisaic shoulders. As to the post-New Testament developments of Judaism they know nothing; and they preach to their people as though the less attractive beliefs of Old or New Testament times contained the sum total of the Jewish religion for the last two thousand years. And all these things are doubly abominable when they occur in Sunday School lessons to the young.*

Today humanity is spiritually homeless as the Jewish people have been geographically homeless; we cannot go back to the world of 1939; we must go forward or perish. Sir William Beveridge has denounced the giants of ignorance and squalor, of idleness and want. But we can only clear them from our path in a healthy society. The giant of antisemitism is as dangerous an enemy, when we turn to the task of creating that society, as any that we shall meet. For our own sakes we must clear him from our path. But a healthy society is also a society in which men do justly one with another. And antisemitism is a giant we must slay also for the sake of the victims, for the sake of the Jews.

Like all men they have their faults; perverted by

*See Bibliography No. 3 at end.

the distortions of a unique history, some faults they show perhaps more frequently than others; but because of that history they are, perhaps, more forgivable than the faults of others; among them there are good and bad as among all others. But like all other peoples, also, they have a contribution to make peculiarly their own. Before the world can be healed we shall need all that the British can give, all that the American, the Frenchman, the Chinese, and men of good will in every nation can offer. In the end we shall need the contributions of the German and the Japanese. And the Jews also have their gifts to bring to the healing of the nations and the enrichment of men.

BIBLIOGRAPHY No. 1

BOOKS ON ANTISEMITISM

In a book of this length I could not possibly cover all aspects of the subject. In particular readers may feel: "but he hasn't explained why Jews have been so unpopular for thousands of years and among all peoples." Here I try to remedy this omission, as well as to deal with modern aspects of the problem.

THE DEVIL AND THE JEW. The Medieval Conception of the Jew and its relation to Modern Antisemitism.　　　　　Joshua Trachtenburg. Yale University Press, 1943.

THE GREAT HATRED.　　　　　Maurice Samuel. Alfred A. Knopf, Inc., 1940.

JEWS IN A GENTILE WORLD.
　　　　The Problem of Antisemitism.
　　　　Isacque Graeber and Steuart Henderson Britt.
　　　　The Macmillan Company, 1942.

INTERNATIONAL ASPECTS OF GERMAN RACIAL POLICIES.
　　　　Oscar I. Janowsky and Melvin M. Fagen.
　　　　Oxford University Press, 1937.

BIBLIOGRAPHY No. 2

BOOKS ABOUT THE JEWS

THE JEWISH CONTRIBUTION TO CIVILIZATION.
　　　　Harper & Brothers, 1940.　　　　Cecil Roth.

THE JEWISH FATE AND FUTURE.　　　　Arthur Ruppin.
　　　　The Macmillan Company, 1940.

THE JEW AND HIS NEIGHBOUR. A Study of the Causes of
    Antisemitism.   James Parkes.
        The Macmillan Co. of Canada, Ltd., 1939.

BIBLIOGRAPHY No. 3

BOOKS ABOUT JUDAISM

THE OLD TESTAMENT AND AFTER.   C. Montefiore.
    The Macmillan Company, 1923.

THE PHARISEES.   Travers Herford.
    The Macmillan Company, 1924.

JESUS AND THE LAW OF MOSES.   B. H. Branscomb.
    Harper & Brothers, 1930.

THE TEACHING OF JESUS.   T. W. Manson.
    The Macmillan Company, 1932.

THE ESSENCE OF JUDAISM.   Leo Baeck.
    The Macmillan Company, 1936.

THUS RELIGION GROWS: The Story of Judaism.
                     Morris Goldstein.
    Longmans Green and Co., Inc., 1936.

THE WISDOM OF ISRAEL.   Edited by Lewis Browne.
    Random House, Inc., 1945.

INDEX

Alexander II, 25, 66

Alexander III, 25, 27

Alliance Israelite Universelle, 28, 29, 32, 75

Anglo-German Fellowship, 54

Antisemitism in 19th century, 4

Antisemitism, legal attack on, 79, 142 f.

Antisemitism, nature of, 63

Arabs, The, 60, 135

Assimilation, 74

Austria-Hungary, 11 ff., 70, 71 f, 76

Bamberger, L., 9 f.

Bismarck, 5 ff.

Black Hundreds, 30

Black Market, 116

Bleichroder, 9

Bloch, J., 17

Bontoux, 13, 14

British Union of Fascists, 55, 59, 78

Brafman, J., 32

Cagoulards, The, 59

Chamberlain, H. S., 49

Cherevin, P. A., 32

Chosen People, The, 94

Churches, responsibility of, 145

Churchill, Mr., 140

Coughlin, Fr., 59

Degrelle, L., 59

Dialogue aux Enfers, 39

Displacement, 86

Dreyfus, A., 21 f.

Drumont, E., 20, 21

Eisenmenger, J. A., 14

Emancipation, 5, 67 ff.

England, 19, 65, 74, 75, 76

Errington, H., 89

France, 9, 13, 24 ff., 128

French Revolution, 8

Freidberg, Emil v., 15

Freidberg, H. v., 16

Freidenthal, K. R., 15

Germany, 5 ff., 76
    See Nazis

Gobineau, Count de, 48

Goedsche, H., 42

Goethe, 49

Gougenot des Mousseaux, 70

Hitler, A., 18, 141. *See* Nazis

Hirsch, Baron de, 75

Hungary, 14, 57, 58, 124

Indians, 90

Italy, 19, 58

Jesus Christ, 49, 95, 98

Jewish argumentativeness, 124
    clannishness, 116, 125
    concentration, 106, 113
    criminality, 117, 118
    foreignness, 103, 126 f.
    ordinariness, 112
    sensitivity, 129, 130

Jews and agriculture, 113
    catering, 115
    clothing, 115
    education, 123 ff.
    entertainment, 104
    law, 113
    medicine, 113
    small business, 115
    usury, 64, 114, 120

Jews and Christians, Societies of, 143, 144

Joint Distribution Committee, 77

Judaism, 94 ff., 120 ff.

Kahal, The, 28 f.

Kulturkampf, The, 8, 10

150

Lasker, E., 9 f.
Law, Jewish attitude to, 100
Leeds, 116
Londoners, The, 90
Lueger, Karl, 18, 50
Lutostansky, H., 28

Maria Theresa, Archduchess, 13
Middle Ages, The, 64
Middle Class, The, 2
Morning Post, The, 37, 38
Mosley, Sir O., 55 f., 58
Moyne, Lord, 119, 140
Mussert, 59
Mussolini, 56, 58, 60

National Home, The, 95, 111, 124, 134
Nazis, The, 45 ff., 78
Nazi antisemitic organizations, 51, 108
Napoleon, Louis, 3, 39, 40
Negroes, 91
Nicholas II, 27, 29, 30
Nilus, S., 33

Old Testament, 63
Onody, G. v., 14
Orgeyevsky, General, 32, 33

Pale of Settlement, The, 24
Philippe, M., 35
Pobyedonostsev, C. P., 26
Poland, 54, 57, 77, 111
Press, Jews and the, 39, 40, 70
Projection, 84
Protocols, The, 27, 30, 32 ff., 79, 118

Quisling, V., 59

Rabbis, The, 97 ff.
Rachkovsky, General, 33
Rationalization, 86
Reform Bill, 1, 2

Refugees from Germany, 77 ff.
Refugees from Russia, 74 f., 78
Renan, E., 49
Retcliffe, Sir J., 42 ff.
Ritual Murder accusation, 14, 99
Rohling, Augustus, 14, 15, 16, 17
Roman Empire, The, 66, 85, 107, 120
Rothschilds, The, 13, 69, 76
Rumania, 56, 57, 59, 72, 77
Russia, 23 ff., 71, 100, 108

Scapegoat, 85, 132
Sephardic, 121
Sincere, Ernest, 44
Socialists and antisemitism, 16, 119
South Africa, 57
South America, 75
Stahl, F. J., 15
Stoecker, A., 10
Stolypin, P. A., 33 f.
Strangers, Jewish attitude to, 96
Syria, 135, 138

Talmud, The, 14, 97, 113, 121
Tertullian, 85
Times, The, 38, 140 f.
Tisza Eszlar, 14
Toussenel, 70
Treitschke, H. v., 11
Trotsky, L., 27

Union Générale, 13
U.S.A., The, 60, 73, 111

von Rath, murder of, 77

Wigram, Major, 89

Zerboni di Sporetti, Ritter v., 13

ABOUT PELICANS

We have long planned a companion series to PEN-
GUIN BOOKS and with the end of paper rationing we
have now launched the PELICAN BOOKS. These will
be nonfiction and on the widest variety of subjects,
such as science, economics, psychology, philosophy, an-
thropology, sociology, the arts, and contemporary
problems both local and international. PELICAN is
the trade name of a similar and very successful series
established by the English Penguin Company, which
introduced authors of such world reputation as Ber-
nard Shaw, Julian Huxley, H. G. Wells, R. H. Tawney,
Frederick Lewis Allen, Sigmund Freud, A. N. White-
head, Margaret Mead.

In our selection of titles we aim to satisfy specific
American requirements through the publication of
books of an authoritative kind by the authors best
qualified to introduce or explain their subject to the
interested layman. We believe in the internationaliza-
tion of ideas and, more, that the American public will
welcome the chance of being able to read, for the first
time at 25c, what the leading experts have to say.

WATCH FOR THIS SYMBOL

PELICANS are now available through bookstores and all other outlets which carry PENGUINS, and new batches will come out at regular intervals.

FIRST PELICAN RELEASES

P 1 PUBLIC OPINION *by Walter Lippmann*

P 2 PATTERNS OF CULTURE *by Ruth Benedict*

P 3 YOU AND MUSIC *by Christian Darnton*

P 4 THE BIRTH AND DEATH OF THE SUN
by George Gamow

P 5 AN ENEMY OF THE PEOPLE: ANTISEMITISM
by James Parkes

P 6 WHAT HAPPENED IN HISTORY
by Gordon Childe

P 7 THE PHYSIOLOGY OF SEX
by Kenneth Walker

P 8 MATHEMATICIAN'S DELIGHT
by W. W. Sawyer

P 9 THE WEATHER *by George H. Kimble*
and Raymond Bush

P 10 AMERICA'S ROLE IN THE WORLD ECONOMY
by Alvin H. Hansen

WATCH ALSO FOR:

HEREDITY, RACE, AND SOCIETY
by Professors L. C. Dunn and T. Dobzhansky

THE STORY OF HUMAN BIRTH
by Dr. A. F. Guttmacher

PHILOSOPHY IN A NEW KEY
by Susanne K. Langer

BALLET *by Arnold Haskell*